BRINGING UP
Bookmonsters

BRINGING UP
Bookmonsters

The Joyful Way to Turn Your Child into a Fearless, Ravenous Reader

AMBER ANKOWSKI, PhD
ANDY ANKOWSKI

THE EXPERIMENT

NEW YORK

BRINGING UP BOOKMONSTERS: *The Joyful Way to Turn Your Child into a Fearless, Ravenous Reader*

Copyright © 2021 by Amber Ankowski, PhD, and Andy Ankowski
Illustrations © 2021 by Franco Zacharzewski

The Experiment, LLC
220 East 23rd Street, Suite 600
New York, NY 10010-4658
theexperimentpublishing.com

THE EXPERIMENT and its colophon are registered trademarks of The Experiment, LLC. Many of the designations used by manufacturers and sellers to distinguish their products are claimed as trademarks. Where those designations appear in this book and The Experiment was aware of a trademark claim, the designations have been capitalized.

The Experiment's books are available at special discounts when purchased in bulk for premiums and sales promotions as well as for fund-raising or educational use. For details, contact us at info@theexperimentpublishing.com.

Library of Congress Cataloging-in-Publication Data

Names: Ankowski, Amber, author. | Ankowski, Andy, author.
Title: Bringing up bookmonsters : the joyful way to turn your child into a
    fearless, ravenous reader / Amber Ankowski, PhD, Andy Ankowski.
Description: New York : The Experiment, 2021. | Includes index.
Identifiers: LCCN 2021000263 (print) | LCCN 2021000264 (ebook) | ISBN
    9781615195862 (paperback) | ISBN 9781615195879 (ebook)
Subjects: LCSH: Reading--Parent participation. | Reading promotion. |
    Children--Books and reading.
Classification: LCC LB1050.2 .A55 2021 (print) | LCC LB1050.2 (ebook) |
    DDC 372.4--dc23
LC record available at https://lccn.loc.gov/2021000263
LC ebook record available at https://lccn.loc.gov/2021000264

ISBN 978-1-61519-586-2
Ebook ISBN 978-1-61519-587-9

Cover and text design, and cover illustration, by Jack Dunnington
Author photograph by Hyla Hedgepeth

Manufactured in the United States of America

First printing April 2021
10 9 8 7 6 5 4 3 2 1

For our all-time favorite bookmonsters,
Sammy, Freddy, and Millie

Contents

The Bookmonster Right Under Your Nose

Cover yourself in khaki and throw on one of those big, round explorer hats. Because we're about to go on an adventure.

Past mountains of dirty laundry . . .

Across carpets booby-trapped with tiny toy landmines . . .

And deep into the lair of the legendary, elusive creature known as the bookmonster!

Ah yes, the bookmonster. If you've not yet heard the tales of this ambitious and adorable species, here are a few important facts about bookmonsters:

1. They may be small in stature, but they are full of confidence.

2. They love to learn and frequently have the grades to prove it.

3. They are curious, imaginative, and able to keep themselves entertained for hours.

Oh, and before we go any further, there's one more thing about bookmonsters that you really ought to know: There has been a bookmonster hiding *inside your child* since birth. And this book—the one you are reading right now—will show you exactly how to bring it out!

About your bookmonster

As a parent, you want your child to become an excellent reader, an A student, and a successful, thriving adult. But that sounds like a whole lot of work for you, huh? Well the good news is, it doesn't have to be. Because if we can somehow help our kids not only learn to read but also learn to love reading, they'll be poised to achieve academic, work, and life success—all on their own.

That's what bringing up a bookmonster is all about.

But, you may be wondering, why on earth would I want my child to be a *monster*? Monsters are rowdy. Messy. Loud. And completely uncontrollable. To that we say, well, yeah. You've got a point there.

But when you think about it, isn't your kid already like that a lot of the time anyway?

Kids are often bursting at the seams with more energy than we parents would sometimes prefer. That's why we're constantly having to clean up their messes, shush their shouting matches, and kiss their bumps and bruises. But if you can help these crazy little kids become *bookmonsters*—children who have developed a fearless, joyful, and ravenous love of *reading*—you'll have successfully redirected a healthy chunk of that excess enthusiasm into something surprisingly peaceful and incredibly important.

How important? Well, consider this.

Learning to read is a life-changing development in every child's life. Once kids discover how to crack that code of previously indecipherable letters, numbers, and punctuation marks, they become more powerful and independent than ever before. They can treat themselves to a reading of any book they want, any time they want it. They can figure out if a restaurant serves chocolate milk, or just plain old white milk, without having to ask. And they can make it impossible for us parents to keep secrets simply by spelling words like B-E-D-T-I-M-E right in front of them.

But these basic language and literacy skills are only the beginning.

Remember that a bookmonster doesn't just know how to read—a bookmonster absolutely adores reading. And it's that insatiable appetite for the written word that can truly transform your child's entire developmental trajectory. Becoming a bookmonster will let your child experience the immediate effects of morphing into a book-devouring animal with mad reading abilities right now, plus continue to benefit your child in all sorts of ways throughout life. That's because bookmonsters commonly experience higher levels of rewarding stuff like:

Academic success

Kids who love language and books will learn to read well before their non-book-loving peers, giving them a major leg up when starting school. Research shows that kids who have a head start early on in school frequently maintain it throughout later grades. And being a great reader will benefit your child not only in English classes but in learning *every other* subject, too.

Self-esteem

Getting good grades in school, receiving positive attention from parents, and having confidence in their ability to learn whatever they want by simply reading about it will help kids feel pretty great about themselves.

Social and emotional development

The more experience kids get reading about characters who feel and express a range of emotions, the more prepared they'll be to develop high-level social skills like empathy.

Imagination

Being a bookmonster gives your child's imagination plenty of practice. Knowing how to transform words written on a page into entire imaginary worlds in your mind is a skill that transfers to lots of other things in life—like envisioning the steps you'll take to fix a faucet, dreaming up an amazing new smoothie flavor, or figuring out which job will make you happiest.

Relationship satisfaction

When you invest time and energy in raising your kid as a bookmonster, it creates a meaningful parent-child bond that can become a blueprint for your little one's ability to form healthy relationships in the future.

Life success

Starting kids off on the right foot with strong literacy skills increases the likelihood that they'll earn higher degrees and hold higher paying jobs. They will also feel happier, freer, and more fulfilled. What could be more satisfying than that?

Teaching your child to read is a nice goal, but an even better one is showing your child how to be a creative critical thinker. And the awesome news is that by bringing your kid up as a bookmonster, you will automatically be doing both.

About your journey

Chances are, you picked up this book because you're interested in the all-important, ultra-serious, and thoroughly terrifying task of Teaching Your Child to Read. Think that sounds a bit over-the-top and intimidating? So do we. But if you've perused any of the other books on children's literacy out there, you may have noticed that it's a fairly typical point of view. Most other resources make teaching children to read seem overly difficult and technical. They make you think that you need worksheets and flashcards, book lists and lesson plans—and above all, hours and hours (and hours) of effort.

But bookmonsters don't need any of that stuff.

Our secret for raising kids who learn to talk early, read easily, and love learning is also stress and worry free. You won't find anything that resembles formal instruction in this book, because what parent has the time or energy to sit down for formal instruction with their kids even once, much less several times a week? Not us! Not you! And in our experience, kids can smell formal instruction coming a mile away—and will do absolutely whatever it takes to avoid it. *What. Ever. It. Takes.*

Fortunately, with the bookmonster method, your kid will never see their reading lessons coming. That's because when you're raising a bookmonster, literacy emerges naturally. By focusing on fun and regularly incorporating books, reading, and conversation into your family's everyday activities, you'll see your child constantly building skills without even realizing it. And you'll be helping them without it ever feeling like a chore. Even chapters toward the end of this book that cover more technical aspects of language can be used with kids of all ages in casual, everyday situations.

But before we get to all that, let's forget about your child for just a second and talk about *you* instead. So please indulge us and answer these two questions:

1. Are you an adult who enjoys reading?
2. Do you have fond memories of reading books as a kid?

Got your answers ready? Good.

If you're like most people, the answers you gave are probably very closely related. People who say they love to read now also commonly have great memories of doing so during childhood—remembering how a parent would read to them, how they'd check out big bags of books at the library, or how they'd spend several hours a day reading over summer breaks. This makes sense, right? If you enjoyed something like reading as a kid, the odds are pretty good you'd still enjoy it as an adult. (Unless you loved eating boogers as a kid. Hopefully you aren't still into that.)

Child development studies support this same idea. One group of researchers followed parents and kids over a five-year period, tracking how much time parents spent teaching literacy skills to their kids versus simply reading to them. What they found is that children whose parents engaged in more explicit literacy instruction—aka "teaching them to read"—scored highest on a reading test in first grade. No surprise there, right? But here's what was surprising: by the third grade, the amount of teaching parents did no longer mattered. Instead, kids who were read to most often were the ones with the best scores.

So what do this study and the little quiz you took right before it tell us about the best way to raise a successful reader? To us, it's the secret of the whole thing . . .

The more *joyful* you make reading, the more *excited* your child will be to read.

The information in this book will empower you with everything you need to know about how kids actually learn to read, and how you can easily incorporate literacy-rich activities into your daily life— whether you liked to read as a kid or not. And because the most important ingredient to raising a bookmonster is entertaining, enjoyable fun, you'll find a whole lot of that, too! Although every activity we suggest in the following pages will help your child build language and literacy skills, none of them will feel like work. We're talking happiness, not homework. Games, not groans. Crack-ups, not cram sessions. Remember to treat your journey that way, and you'll be raising a little bookmonster—and strengthening your bond with your child—before you know it.

About your guides

When you're setting out on a quest to discover, care for, and unleash your child's inner bookmonster, you shouldn't have to do it alone. And with this book, you won't have to.

With you every step of the way will be Amber Ankowski, PhD, a professor of developmental psychology whose specialty is teaching children's language development, and Andy Ankowski, her advertising writer husband whose specialty is making jokes that small children think are funny. Together, we speak, teach, and write about the most effective parenting techniques around. And when we're not doing that, we're conducting research at home—on three little bookmonsters of our own!

All three of our kids have displayed telltale bookmonster characteristics—they were early talkers, consider books to be some of their very favorite toys, and learned to read by the age of five. All that and we don't even own a single flashcard. At least we don't think we do . . . this place is a freakin' mess. (Did we mention we have three kids? Yes? Oh good.)

One of the coolest things about being the parents of multiple bookmonsters is that we've been able to observe how each attacks reading in a unique way. Our eldest daughter devours any book she can get her hands on, including chapter books well above her grade level. Our son goes after books that have fun with language—rhymes, jokes, and nonsense words really get him giggling. And our youngest girl started forcibly shoving books in our faces at the age of one, yelling "Booo" and plunking herself onto our laps until we'd read to her at pretty much all hours of the day. Despite having different ways of showing it, they are all bookmonsters. And once you begin bringing up bookmonsters of your own, you too will marvel at the unique ways your children show off their own love of language and literacy.

So make sure your reading lamp is fully operational, and your fingertips are fully licked. Then turn the page . . . and let the bookmonster hunt begin!

PART I

Giving Birth to Your Bookmonster

Most people agree that giving birth to a baby is grueling, painful, and exhausting work. But if you think that bringing a child who knows how to read into the world has to feel the same way, think again! The following pages will show you how easy "giving birth" to a bookmonster can be. We'll break down the basic ways that you communicate with your child, including talking, listening, gesturing, and reading together, and show how you can use each of them to set your child up for reading success. You can use these tips as soon as your baby is born, or at any time afterward—because it's never too early or too late to start bringing out your child's inner bookmonster. And the best part is, none of these strategies will feel anything like labor!

Anatomy of a Bookmonster

Bird. Fish. Deer. Bookmonster. It doesn't matter what kind of creature you're hunting—you'll never find it unless you know exactly what you're looking for. So your first step in bringing up a bookmonster should begin right here. Think of the next few pages as your handy-dandy field guide to identifying the many unique features of the super-literate species your child will soon become.

Read it. Study it. And get ready for your little one to live it.

Scientific Name:

Devoroscriptum monstrosus ("monstrous devourer of letters")

Common Names:

Bookmonster, Bookworm, Independent Reader, Excellent Student, Brainiac, Creative Kid, Possessor of Above-Average Vocabulary, The Great Communicator, Li'l Smartypants, Your Pride and Joy

Identifying Characteristics:

1. BRAINS that are super smart and ready for school

Although babies begin life with most of the neurons they will ever have, the brain isn't even close to finished developing at birth. Instead, during the first decade of life and beyond, the brain undergoes an extensive process of acquiring efficient, accurate connections between neurons that facilitate increasingly complex cognition. In other words, your child's brain still has a lot of growing to do! This intricate, dynamic growing process is how the brain sets itself up for adultlike thinking. And it's also totally dependent upon the experiences a child has.

All kinds of life experiences can affect how a child acts—from dietary changes to everyday stress to traumatic events and much more. But what you may not realize is that these environmental influences also affect a child's physical brain development. That means that the things we expose kids to now can affect the way they think throughout their entire lives. For example, fetuses and young children who are exposed to cigarette smoke show distinct differences in their brains that are linked to increased problem behavior as early as preschool.

Even the seemingly insignificant ways we talk, read, and otherwise interact with kids can greatly influence the way they think and behave throughout their entire lives. That's why making the decision to raise a bookmonster is so important. Learning to read requires multiple areas of your child's brain to work together in new ways, including visual areas that decipher written symbols, auditory areas that decode letter sounds, linguistic areas that coordinate written information with spoken vocabulary, and conceptual areas that relate written content with stored knowledge. It's really a whole-brain workout!

2. EYES eagerly seeking out opportunities to learn

Babies emerge from the womb with a natural predisposition to learn from others. Within hours of being born, they can already mimic your facial expressions. And by six weeks old, they can remember and continue to imitate specific faces you've made, even when you're not around. These helpless-looking little balls of baby fat truly have far greater capabilities than meet the eye. They watch you with alert, inquisitive eyes from the very start, absorbing everything and learning increasingly advanced lessons as they grow.

When kids finally come to realize that the lines and squiggles they see in books are meaningful, it's a wondrous experience. Kids suddenly have access to a whole new world of information and are aware that they are surrounded by more interesting ideas and stories than they ever knew. We can't really remember what it was like back when we experienced it ourselves, but we imagine that it must be something like an infant's first taste of real food. For the longest time all they get to eat is mushed up vegetables in a single flavor. Then suddenly they get a taste of pizza and realize with a shocking start that the world is a place full of sensational flavors—so fork them over, folks!

As soon as children awaken to the joy of language and print, they eagerly eyeball words wherever they can be found, and apply their natural learning mechanisms to the task of becoming full-fledged bookmonsters.

3. EARS pricked up and excellent at listening

We know as well as anybody how hard it can be to get kids to listen. We could yell "Pick up these toys," "Wash your hands," or "Time for bed" at the top of our lungs for hours without any of our children even batting an eye. (Yet the instant we whisper "chocolate," they come running—what's up with that?) Well, one cool thing about bookmonsters is that they tend to be somewhat less terrible at listening to you than the average kid.

How's that work exactly? Each time you crack open a book and share it with your child, you're engaging in an activity that requires them to listen carefully to get the most out of the story. But even more important, you're also giving them the priceless gift of your love and attention. By pairing precious cuddles with the act of sitting still and concentrating, you're helping them feel good about a skill that will prove to be incredibly valuable to them all throughout life. Bookmonsters aren't naturally calmer or more studious than other kids. They just get more practice at it. And that practice has the potential to pay off big-time.

4. MOUTHS filled with an ever-expanding vocabulary

Sorry (not sorry), but bookmonsters aren't the kind of creatures that are seen and not heard. They've got great big booming vocabularies that simply cannot be stifled. Even our son, who happens to be a super quiet guy, can really get going when the subject is something he cares about—like robots, or bacon, or pie. (You know, the good stuff in life.) When kids are exposed to lots of books and fun literary interactions like the ones you'll find in this book, they'll develop enormous vocabularies, gain skills in expressing their thoughts and feelings, and generally become really great conversation partners.

So sit back and enjoy. Once you get used to the volume, there's really no cuter sound than your bookmonster's voice.

5. HEARTS brimming with a love of books (and people)

The idea that your bookmonsters will be totally, completely, head-over-heels in love with reading should come as no surprise. After all, loving books is what bookmonsters do best. But you may not realize that all the page-perusing your kid will soon be doing can help them feel more compassionate toward other people as well.

You see, understanding stories requires you to take on different characters' perspectives, comprehending their feelings to see the motivations for their actions. This is true for all stories, from brief picture books to lengthy adult novels. That's why frequent readers exhibit superior empathy skills throughout life. Children who are read to more often develop better skills at relating to others at earlier ages. And adults who read more frequently tend to be more compassionate as well. Since understanding other people's perspectives is an important prerequisite to successful social interaction, this bodes well for your kiddo's ability to form healthy relationships on the playground, at the office, and eventually in their water aerobics class at the senior center.

Reading gives kids a chance to step into the shoes of people very different from themselves, experiencing challenges and joys far removed from their everyday lives. They also get to do some really cool stuff they otherwise would only dream of. Like rocketing to meet the moon's resident cheese monster in *Charlie and the Cheese Monster* by Justin C. H. Birch, or single-handedly leading a full-fledged marching band in *Olivia Forms a Band* by Ian Falconer, or manufacturing an airplane out of household objects and performing in an air show in *Violet the Pilot* by Steve Breen. With books, the possibilities are boundless—just like the love your child will feel for them.

6. ARMS strong enough to tote lots of books

Bookmonsters are super strong—from carrying so many books, of course!

Although let's be completely honest here. While it's true that bookmonsters are very often found with books in their arms, the joke is sort of on us here, since we adults are the ones who end up lugging ridiculously heavy bagfuls of books from the library on a regular basis. But trust us, the lifetime of benefits you're delivering to your bookmonsters will make those sore biceps worth it.

7. HANDS ready to write

From gesturing to get their point across before they can even speak, to flipping pages faster than you can say "encyclopedia," to penning their own poems and essays, bookmonsters are always active with their hands. The joy they experience while consuming book after book quite often leads to a natural, irrepressible desire to express themselves—by becoming the authors of their very own creative works!

2

The Perfect Bookmonster Call

When you're fishing, you push hooks through slimy, wriggling, dirt-covered worm bodies with your bare hands. When you're hunting, you douse yourself in deer urine. Both are effective ways of attracting prey, but also super gross. Fortunately for you, luring the bookmonster out of your bambino doesn't have to be disgusting at all. That's because the absolute best bookmonster call ever invented is . . .

(Are you ready for it?)

Your voice! Specifically, it's your voice speaking words. Lots and lots and lots and *lots* of words.

Bookmonsters are instinctively drawn to words. They just can't get enough of them. So the more words you say to your child, and the earlier in life you start saying them, the sooner you'll have a hungry little bookmonster on your hands. The science behind this is pretty simple: The more words kids hear, the more words they'll understand. The more words they understand, the more easily they'll recognize them when they see them in print. The more words they read in print, the more *new* words they'll discover, learn, and understand. And so on, and so forth, for the rest of their book-loving lives.

So truly, the first and most important thing you can do to help young children learn to read is to have tons of conversations with them. And we do mean tons. Like, so many conversations that your throat is scratchy and you're sick of hearing your own voice and you don't even have anything else to say, but you keep on talking anyway.

At the beginning of your child's life, the specific content of your conversations is not all that important. You can talk about changing a diaper, eating spoonfuls of mushy peas, snapping buckles in a stroller, seeing a squirrel climb a tree, how wonderful hugs and kisses are, or how military overspending and oppressive taxation contributed to the fall of the Roman Empire. (You know, whatever's on your mind.) Just make sure your child hears lots of great, meaty language throughout the day. Your bookmonsters will automatically do the rest—sinking their tiny teeth into it, gobbling it right up, and using it to grow a truly impressive vocabulary.

What if you're not a big talker? Or don't believe that your voice is really the best bookmonster call ever? Or just like doing things the hard way? Well, some people like to shove their entire arms into underwater mud holes and use them as bait for catching catfish. We're not gonna try to stop them either.

But consider this: The number of words children hear in the first few years of life can affect them far longer than you might expect. Here's why:

1. Researchers counting up the number of words parents say to their children in ordinary home life situations have estimated that some kids hear up to *thirty million more words* than others between birth and four years old.

2. Kids who have heard more words significantly outscore their less-spoken-to peers in measures of vocabulary size and school readiness.

3. Children with larger vocabularies and better school readiness on day one of kindergarten (before they've even had a single teacher-led lesson!) tend to earn better grades throughout *all* their school years.

So by the time kindergarten begins, some children have heard far more words than others, and it has a tremendous influence on their long-term academic success. Which means that you—and your voice—have an undeniably important job to do.

So get talking!

Seriously, put down this book and start a convo with your kiddo right this instant. (Unless your child is asleep. In that case, please relish this beautiful parenting break while you have the chance, and start talking after "magic time" is over.) You can even use this book as a prop if you like, discussing the fantastical bookmonster illustration you've just seen. You can talk about how cute it is or how fierce it looks gobbling up the words. You can talk about the specific letters it's eating, or what color you think it should be, or what you would name it if you had it for a pet. Again, the specifics aren't that important. Just that you're chatting, and your child is listening.

Go ahead. We'll wait.

. . .

That was pretty fun, right? We hope so, because it should be fun! In fact, we think fun should always be your number one goal when conversing with your kid. Everyone learns best when they're having fun. Plus, it'll result in the best bonding, too!

But what if your conversation was hampered because you had one or more of the following concerns?

Worried your child is too young?

Rest assured, kids are *never* too young for conversation. The ideal time to start talking your little bookmonsters' ears off is as soon as they're born. But if by chance your child wasn't born yesterday and you're getting a bit of a later start, don't fret. Any time is a great to time to start having tons of conversations—and once you start, remember never to stop! Initially kids won't be able to contribute to the conversation much at all. But over time they'll begin to respond with grunts and groans, then adorable babbling noises, eventually words, and finally full-fledged sentences. Your child will take up more and more of the conversation every day, and the more you talk, the faster it will happen.

Afraid your child won't understand what you're saying?

No matter what age your budding bookmonster is, one thing is certain: Your child *always* understands way more than you think. This is true at every single point in development. Babies are born already recognizing their parents' voices (since they heard them so much in the womb). Toddlers know what you mean when you say "spaghetti" and "burrito" (even though when they say them, they come out sounding like "pasgeddy" and "daboodoob"). And thirty-year-olds still living at home fully comprehend that they really ought to move out of their parents' basements (but just can't even because adulting is soooooo hard).

By the time babies *say* their first word, they already *understand* dozens and dozens of them. So go ahead and assume kids know far more than it seems, and treat them accordingly.

Feel awkwardly like you're talking to yourself?

We're not going to lie. When you start following our advice, you may get some weird looks in public. When our oldest daughter was ready for a big girl bed, we took her to the furniture store to pick one out. Amber and our tiny two-year-old were walking hand in hand through the store, discussing the various available options, when a befuddled salesperson approached Amber, asked, "Who are you talking to?" and swung her head around like a wild, bug-eyed ostrich looking for the answer. No joke. By the look on the salesperson's face, she apparently thought it was more likely that Amber was discussing furniture with an invisible apparition of an interior designer than with her own, 100-percent-visible daughter. But that's just because she, like many people, didn't understand how important interaction is for children's development. Trust us—even if children can't yet respond, they're listening attentively.

Think you have to stick to basic words?

Remember, building a big vocabulary is the goal, so the more different words you use, the more words your child will learn. In fact, parents with larger vocabularies tend to have kids with larger vocabularies. That's because those parents are using their impressive repertoire of words when they talk to their kids. So no matter how big or small your own vocabulary is, you should skip the baby talk, and let your child benefit from hearing all the words you know. (Well, maybe not *all* the words. Save the sailor talk for after bedtime.)

Don't know what you should talk about?

We get that talking all the time might not come naturally to every-body. But remember: 1) It's for your bookmonster's good, 2) Your kid isn't judging your conversational skills like you're on a job interview or a first date, and 3) It really doesn't matter what you say, as long as you're saying something! But if you still want some specific direction, follow these tips for adding more chatter to your child's day.

Describe everything

If you've ever thought you might have what it takes to be a good sports commentator, now's the time to prove it. Pretend the activities you and your child engage in are a sporting event, and your job is to give the play-by-play. The result is that you end up describing everything that's going on around you—what you're doing, why you're doing it, the names of the people, animals, or inanimate objects that happen to be around you while you're doing it, and so on. Doing this helps kids hear more words and learn language to match their experienc-es. This tip is especially useful when your child is too little to fully participate in back-and-forth conversations and you'll be doing much of the talking anyway.

Be a human thesaurus

Kids learn lots of words just by figuring out what they mean from the context of ordinary conversations. But sometimes it's a good idea to teach words more deliberately. If you come across a word that's unusual, confusing, or just strikes you as interesting, take a second to explicitly discuss it with your child. If you see a "caution" sign, you can talk about how big and crazy sounding the word is but that it just means we need to be careful. Or if you're out exploring and see a moth, you can talk about how moths are like butterflies but have darker colors and come out at night. Once you get started you'll be surprised at how naturally it comes, because you know best which words your kid already knows, which words they might be ready to learn, and which new words they might most enjoy discussing.

Appeal to your child's interests

Your child isn't going to get as much out of your conversations if they're a total snoozefest. So keep your child involved and engaged by appealing to their own unique interests. If your kid loves trucks, point out and discuss all the cool-looking heavy machinery in that construction site over there. If your kid responds with, "No, I said I love *ducks*," then say, "My bad," and head to the nearest pond.

Talk about intangibles

Have some conversations about things that are not right in front of your child's face, like activities you've experienced together in the past, things you plan to do in the future, or objects and people not in the room. Since these conversations are more complex than discussing what you can readily see and point to, kids can get more advanced language and literacy development from them.

Schedule some speaking time

If you don't feel like you're getting enough talk time with your child spontaneously throughout the day, try setting up an appointment for some. Having daily, distraction-free family dinners with everyone sitting around the table together gives you an ideal opportunity to talk. And dozens of studies have found that having at least five family dinners per week is associated with all kinds of positive outcomes for kids, including:

- larger vocabularies
- higher reading scores
- greater motivation in school
- better relationships with peers and parents
- healthier eating habits
- fewer instances of eating disorders, obesity, drinking, and drug use
- better emotional well-being and life satisfaction

Plus, there's dessert!

3

Listening to a Bookmonster

Unless you enjoy getting mauled by pets, it's helpful to know the difference between a dog's playful pant and its intimidating growl—and between a cat's "pet me" purr and its "my claws are coming at you" hiss.

But what about the sounds your bookmonster makes? Do you know how to listen for them? Do you recognize what they mean? And do you understand the best ways to respond to them? When you're trying to help children become self-sufficient readers, it's important to keep your ears open for every sound they make. Because hidden inside each of your bookmonster's grunts and groans is a great opportunity for you to respond—and for your child to learn.

Here's what we mean: When parents are good, responsive listeners, children develop better language skills more quickly. How? Just think about what happens when you reply to your child's attempts at communicating with you versus when you don't. When you do reply, it probably goes something like this:

Your child says something.
You say something back.
Your child says something again.
You say something back.
And so on, until pretty soon you're having a real, live conversation that you both just might get something valuable from.

When you don't respond, however, it probably goes more like this:

Your child says something.
You ignore it.
Your child wanders off to play with matches and swallow laundry detergent.

Not as good, right?

There's plenty of scientific evidence supporting this idea, too. In one experiment, researchers observed several conversations between parents and children. They noticed that some parents were very responsive when their kid attempted to communicate with them—verbally answering, nodding, smiling, or simply delivering a well-timed touch that showed they were listening. Other parents barely acknowledged their kid's efforts at all. When the researchers compared the children's language development, they found that kids whose parents responded more had larger vocabularies and achieved language milestones like saying first words and sentences at earlier ages.

In another study, nine-month-old children who weren't speaking actual words yet played with their parents for half an hour. Some of the parents were instructed to respond each time their child started "babbling"—making language-like sounds that resemble speech—by speaking, moving closer, smiling, or touching their children. The other parents were told to do those same behaviors, but at random times *not* synced with their babies' vocalizations. The result? Children whose parents provided responses in sync with their vocalizations experienced impressive growth over the brief play session—producing more frequent and linguistically complex babbles at the end than when the experiment started.

If kids' language skills can improve that much from just thirty minutes of thoughtful reactions from parents, imagine what your bookmonster will be able to accomplish when you make listening and responding to them a normal, everyday habit!

Here are some ways to do just that. Check out the following chart for a list of sounds your child could make at different stages in life, what those sounds mean, and ideas for how you can respond to them!

Child's sound	What it means	How to respond
Crying Grunting Burping	These aren't really language sounds but rather babies' first opportunities to practice using their vocal equipment.	Check on them to see what they need. Odds are, it's food, a nap, or a fresh diaper!
Cooing	At around two months old, babies start using vowels only (like "aaah" and "oooh").	Coo right back, Mama and Papa Bird.

Child's sound	What it means	How to respond
Vocal Play	At around four months old, babies first begin to incorporate some consonants into their vocalizations.	This requires more advanced motor movements, so congratulate your little one on all the hard work.
Babbling	Around nine months, babies start alternating consonants and vowels— first in a repetitive fashion ("babababa" and "memememe"), then mixed up ("bawadedoma").	Encourage further sound experimentation by first mimicking the sounds your child is making ("wewewewe"), and then changing them slightly ("woowoowoowoo") to see if your child can follow suit.
Jargon	Babies combine babbling with appropriate intonation (like pretending to talk on the phone and not using any real words, but mimicking the rhythm of conversation).	Take this as a clear cue your child is interested in conversing with you—then do it, saying a sentence or two before pausing to give your babbler a "turn" in the conversation.
Protowords	These are made-up words that the child always uses to mean the same thing, but that don't actually sound like the adult word for that thing (like calling water "baya").	Try to figure out what these protowords mean. Each one you successfully decode makes you that much better at communicating with your kiddo!
First Words	There's a huge age range for when kids say their first words (from about 9 months to 2 years, with an average of 12 months), and it's usually the name of one of their parents.	If it was your name the baby said first, relish this moment. If it was someone else's, remind yourself to say your name a lot more to any future babies you may have.

Dramatic (and profoundly sad) evidence for the immense effect of responding to your child comes from research on the development of children in international orphanages in which there are not enough caregivers to properly attend to the needs of the children. In situations like this, there may be as many as ten children per caregiver—an arrangement that allows the caregiver to address only the most basic requirements of each child, like changing diapers and feeding, all of which is expediently done while leaving the child lying in a crib. Children do not get fed when they feel hungry or changed when their diapers get messy, because they are only given attention when it's their turn. This is starkly different than a typical caregiving situation, in which a baby's cries cause a parent to pick up the child and tend to whatever it needs. Because there is no reliable response when the orphans cry, they learn to stop crying altogether.

If you learn nothing else from this chapter, please understand that your responses are incredibly powerful. The more you respond, the more your child learns. The more your child learns, the more they will talk. The more they talk, the more you will respond. And on and on, in a monstrously magical language development loop.

Don't feel like your kid conversation game is quite up to snuff? Here are some specific tips that can help:

Realize that you can't fake it

Ever caught yourself acting like you were listening to your wee one, but you were really just nodding and tossing out a few random "uh-huh"s, "oh really"s, and "you'll have to ask your mother about that"s? Well, your kid has caught you doing it, too. Children are way smarter than we often give them credit for, including being incredibly adept at reading social cues. To give them the benefits that come with actual, thoughtful responses, you'll have to stop phoning it in (which probably involves not staring at your phone so much).

Show some emotion

Remember, the goal here is to give your child lots of practice talking. So make sure they feel plenty of positive reinforcement that lets them know just how much you love hearing them speak. Smile big, nod enthusiastically, stare in amazement when they tell you something crazy, and laugh long and hard when they crack a joke. It'll show them that you're listening, make them feel appreciated, and be more fun for you, too!

Follow your child's lead

Research shows that kids learn the most from conversations they can control. So talk about things your child is already focused on whenever possible. Like, even if you're super jazzed to unveil a big lesson on letters that you spent all night preparing, but your child is elbow deep in the sandbox, remind yourself to be flexible. Instead of forcing the kid to switch gears and pay attention to the book you're holding, join in the fun yourself! Grab a shovel, giggle about what a mess you two are making, and *then* sprinkle some educational trivia into your playtime talk—"Did you know that sand is actually teensy tiny pieces of rock that got broken down by wind and water over lots and lots of years?" You can always chat about letters later.

Take your kid's questions seriously

We get that children's questions are so common that they've become a joke. *Are we there yet? What's for dinner? How come that man who is totally within earshot of us doesn't have any hair on his big bald head? Why? Why not? Why? Why? Why? Why? Why?* And research confirms that it's not just parents' imaginations. According to one study, kids actively interacting with parents ask an average of about seventy-six information-seeking questions per hour. Yikes! But before you chalk this up to kids just being annoying, remember that this only happens because kids are inherently curious. They're like little scientists trying to figure out the world, and their questions are an invitation for you to help. And your answers do help a lot! Information that kids glean from questions they ask stays with them much better than information that was given to them unprompted. It's kind of flattering, too—when your child asks you a question, it means they actually want to hear what you have to say.

Ask your own questions

Asking your child questions is a great way to encourage interaction. Plus, sometimes you'll hear really entertaining stuff that you'd never expect. Like one time when our three-year-old son told us that a stick he was holding was a balloon gun. We naturally assumed he meant a gun that shot balloons. So it's a good thing we asked, because he informed us that it actually shot "poisonous vanilla cakes for bad guys' birthday parties"—which was a delightfully surprising answer. We know that sometimes it's hard to get kids to answer ordinary, everyday questions like "How was school?" So try more unusual queries like, "What was the funniest thing that happened today?" or "Did you do any particularly interesting or boring assignments in class?" Just remember that questions should be posed as a conversation, not a quiz!

Remember that you're bonding

Responding to your kid promptly and consistently is good for more than language development—it does wonders for their social and emotional development, too. The way you respond is a major factor in determining how attached to you your child will become. And secure attachment predicts lots of positive outcomes for your family, including a better parent-child relationship now and your child's lasting ability to create and maintain higher quality relationships throughout life.

Don't give up

One thing about tiny humans just learning to talk: They don't always pronounce everything perfectly. Kids commonly mispronounce words by repeating a first syllable ("baba" for "bottle"), omitting a consonant from a group of consonants ("pider" for "spider"), forgetting the final consonant of a word ("bu" for "bug"), or omitting a syllable ("bana" for "banana"). And it might take them a long time to enunciate difficult letter sounds like *s*, *f*, *th*, *z*, *v*, and *j*. Sometimes parents freak out and rush to seek intervention because their children can't do it yet, but you can relax. It's totally natural for kids to still be working on their mastery through about eight years old! Instead of worrying about language errors like these, try to focus on how darn cute they are while they last! We've enjoyed some of our kids' mispronunciations so much that they've stuck around. In our house computers are now "compootoobs," humans are "hoomans," and "sleep well" sounds like "sleep way-ull."

But there will inevitably be times when your little one is trying to tell you something, and you can't for the life of you figure out what it is. In those situations, you can either smile and say something vaguely positive, like "Oh really? Wow!" hoping your kid moves on to another thought, or you can try to deduce what exactly it is that your child is attempting to say. If you go the Sherlock Holmes route, here are some strategies that might help.

- Guess ("You saw a bird?" *No.* "You saw a boat?" *No.* "You saw avocado toast?")

- Ask an older sibling (they're usually good at speaking Kid)

- Admit you're having trouble, and ask your child to help ("I'm sorry, kiddo, but I'm having a hard time understanding that one word. Could you describe what it looks like? Do you know another word for it? Can you act it out?")

We'd followed these steps so often with our youngest bookmonster that by the time she was three, she would voluntarily give us synonyms for words we couldn't quite get—before we even had to ask!

Give yourself a break

By now, we think we've impressed upon you just how massively important it is for you to respond to your child. But don't freak out and think that if you fail to speak up every single time your kid opens their mouth they'll be screwed for life. Sometimes both you and your child will need a break—and it will actually be beneficial for your child's development. You see, in addition to talking with you, kids talk to themselves. A lot. Talking to themselves (or what child development professionals call "private speech") is important for language and cognitive development. Children often use it to practice and internalize what they've learned through conversations with you. So the things kids say when they talk to themselves are often more linguistically complex than what they typically say throughout the day. Children use private speech to try out new words and word-forms before they debut them in real interactions, or to guide themselves through particularly difficult tasks. You can sometimes observe children talking to themselves while playing with toys, sitting alone in the car seat, lying in bed before they drift to sleep, and other quiet times. We recommend that you eavesdrop on your child's private speech whenever you can—partly because they probably won't do it forever, but mostly because it's so darn cute!

4

Moving Like a Bookmonster

Chameleons change colors to express their moods. Pufferfish inflate their bodies into big, spiky balls to say "don't eat me." And blue-footed boobies do a crazy, high-strutting dance when they want to attract a mate. Believe it or not, bookmonsters are a lot like each of these animals: When they have something they want to communicate, they get their entire bodies into the act!

That's right. Bookmonsters love to gesture. Although tons of people "talk with their hands" all the time, they almost never consciously think about it. And when people do consider gesturing, they often assume it's just some mindless hand-wagging that makes Italian family reunions more fun.

But there's way more to it than that.

You see, gesturing is really great for your bookmonster's language development. And to hear the entire story about that, you need to start at the beginning (of your kid's life, that is).

The development of gesture

In case you hadn't noticed, babies don't come out of the womb speaking up a storm. That's because developing the ability to control your vocal cords enough to produce actual words is pretty hard! But you know what isn't so tough? Figuring out how to control your hands, limbs, and other big, obvious body parts. That's why young children communicate with you using gestures well before they do it with speech. Here are a few examples.

When kids want to	They might	To mean
Indicate objects	• Make a throwing motion • Bounce their bodies • Sniff	• "Ball" • "Horse" • "Flower"
Make requests	• Raise their arms • Move hands up and down • Pat Mommy's boobies	• "Pick me up" • "Play piano" • "Lunchtime"
Describe things	• Put up their palms • Stretch out their arms • Lick their lips	• "All gone" • "Big" • "Yummy" (which is also about mommy's boobies pretty often, right?)

As you can see, kids use everything at their disposal to get their point across before they can use words, and they employ their whole bodies to make sure their messages are understood. Gesturing is such a natural part of learning and communicating that speakers of all languages around the world do it. Even people who are born blind gesture, despite never seeing the gestures other people produce!

Kids' gestures and vocabularies are connected

Once children start talking, don't expect their gestures to suddenly go away. In fact, researchers have found that there is a consistent relationship between gestures and speech all throughout development. In general, when kids use more gestures, they also say more words.

But why is that?

To answer that question, consider one of the most common gestures you, your child, and everybody else on the planet uses—pointing. Most kiddos begin pointing within a few months of their first birthday, and it's a pretty powerful milestone. That's because pointing marks a major shift in your baby's thinking, showing that they now realize objects in the world can be referred to with words . . . and they want you to tell them what those words are.

Just think about what happens when a young child gestures around you. Let's say you're sitting in the kitchen, and your little monkey starts pointing excitedly toward a banana. You're probably going to respond by talking, saying something like, "Oh, the banana? Do you want a banana?" And then your kid is probably going to start freaking out, nodding, grunting, and attempting to dive headfirst from the high chair directly into the fruit bowl. At this point, you'll surely continue talking, offering reassurances like, "Don't worry, I can get you the banana right now. See, I'm peeling the banana. This banana is going to taste so yummy, isn't it? OK, here's your banana!"

Did you notice how that one little gesture from your child resulted in you saying lots and lots of words? Children's gestures are invitations for you to interact with them, and their gestures in response to your words serve to encourage you to keep on gabbing. A major reason that children who gesture more learn language faster is that they simply hear more of it.

Getting right to the point

What are you, as the parent of a future bookmonster, supposed to do with all this information? Basically this: Make sure you gesture, too!

While you're moving your mouth to expose your child to all the language they need to hear, don't forget to also keep your hands moving. Parents who gesture a lot tend to have kids who learn language faster, not only because the little ones learn to gesture more themselves but also because the parents' gestures help the kids identify what words mean. Think about the task of learning words. It's hard because there is so much a single word might refer to. When your baby hears you use the word "cup" while you're sitting at dinner, it could mean any number of things related to what's going on. It could refer to the food, the act of eating, the table, a fork, the family dog scrounging for scraps on the floor, the time of day—the list goes on. But when you point to the cup, wag it around, or otherwise indicate it with your gestures as you're talking, it helps your child narrow down what "cup" might mean, and makes learning the word much easier.

Try to communicate with your hands as well as your mouth, and you'll give your bookmonster a real leg up.

How to make book reading a full-body workout

What if gesturing doesn't come naturally to you, and being a "hand talker" in your everyday conversations just isn't your thing? Don't worry! Reading aloud is the perfect time to incorporate more language-boosting gestures into your interactions with your bookmonster. After all, you'll have your child's attention, you'll have a specific thing you're gesturing toward (the book, obviously), and you'll have these simple ideas for exactly how to do it:

Indicate illustrations

One thing that kids learn during book reading is about the pictures themselves—namely that they are a symbol or representation of the thing and not the object itself. You may have observed kids trying to figure this out firsthand if you've ever had the experience of watching a young child try to pet a picture of a dog or lick a picture of an ice cream cone. Our own littlest bookmonster went through an endearing phase of saying hi to all the people in the pictures as we read. Even into the preschool years, kids persist in misunderstandings about illustrations—like believing that a picture of a popsicle might be cold to the touch. This behavior is completely normal and nothing to worry about, and your child will naturally learn to understand pictures as symbols over time. But even before that happens, you can use your gestures to call attention to the illustrations, which will boost story comprehension, help your kid understand what the words you're reading refer to, and clarify how the pictures relate to the text. For example, simply pointing to characters like Piggie or Gerald as they say their lines of dialogue in *I Will Take a Nap!* by Mo Willems can help kids understand how the characters they see relate to the dialogue you're describing.

Point to print

Research analyzing children's behavior during reading time shows that kids pay little attention to print without guidance. That means that if you don't encourage your bookmonster to look at the letters and words, they might miss them altogether. An easy way to do that is by occasionally running your finger underneath the text as you're reading. This will help your child learn many important book basics, including that the print tells the story you're saying and that words are always read in the same direction—like left-to-right rows in English, and top-to-bottom columns in Japanese.

Pantomime verbs

Verbs are particularly hard for kids to learn, because they're not touchable or permanent. For example, a "jump rope" is always there to look at and point to, but a "jump" is only there for the split second you're doing it. So give your kid more experience with verbs and a better understanding of their meanings when you encounter them in stories. If you're reading Jim Aylesworth's retelling of *The Gingerbread Man*, act out "mixing" and "rolling" the dough, and help your kid put their "little hands" on their "little hips" each time the Gingerbread Man speaks—it's about the sweetest thing you'll see all day!

Act out songs

Whether you're reading lyrics in a book or just singing for fun, adding gestures to your songs automatically makes them more instructive and enjoyable. You can sing children's songs that contain specific moves to perform, like "The Hokey Pokey" or "The Itsy Bitsy Spider," or put your own spin on the classics—we enjoy finishing "Where Is Thumbkin?" by chasing the kids with tickle fingers during the final "Run away!" line. You can also make up your own songs and gestures to fit any situation or mood your family finds itself in. Amber's sister has an original ditty called "Stirring the Pot," which mainly involves her singing those three words over and over as she stirs macaroni noodles, chicken soup, or whatever she's making. It's simple, but it makes cooking just a little more memorable. (And her kids *totally* know what a pot is now.)

How Gesture Helps Babies Use Words Before They Even Speak

Wish you could know exactly what your newborn was thinking? Well, infants who learn "baby sign" can tell you! Even though they may be many months away from saying their first word out loud, your little ones most likely understand a whole bunch of the words you say every day. By teaching them how a few simple hand movements can correspond with those words, they can start showing you what they know!

Unlike normal gestures that speakers make up on the fly while talking, baby sign uses a system of gestures that always mean the same thing. For example, a two-handed gesture that mimics the hand motions of milking a cow could be used to mean "milk," and repetitively opening and closing one hand like a mouth could be used to mean "duck." You can use standardized signs based on American Sign Language that you find in a baby sign book, which may be especially useful if your child will be attending a childcare facility that uses ASL-based signs and you want to maintain consistency at home. Or if you just want a simple way to understand things like whether your kiddo has an empty stomach or a full diaper, you can create personalized movements for your own family's use. The specific signs you use don't matter too much, as long as you consistently pair the same gesture with the same word. To start using baby sign, just act out your chosen gesture each time you say its word to your child, and your child naturally learns that the hand movement is a sign for the word.

Sometimes people are reluctant to use baby sign because they think that if their child has gestures to communicate with, they won't be as motivated to learn spoken words. But numerous studies have shown that the opposite is true. This is why bookmonsters love baby sign! It gives them valuable practice with language at the earliest possible age, which will only help them as they grow to become confident talkers, and then super-skilled readers!

5

The Right Time to Read to a Bookmonster

Fireflies only show up around dusk during the warmest couple months of the year. Koalas are awake and active for as little as two hours each day. And the Braken Bat Cave Meshweaver Spider once went thirty years without being spotted. To catch a glimpse of some animals, your timing has to be perfect.

Sightings of bookmonsters enjoying books, on the other hand, are about as common as they come—happening morning, noon, and night every winter, spring, summer, and fall. So if you've ever wondered when you should read to your child, the truth is that there isn't a single best time. There are tons of them. First thing when you wake up? Yes. Right before you go to bed? You bet. Every hour on the hour seven days a week? If your kid wants it—and your voice can handle it—why not?

Reading often with your child is a massively important part of getting them to love reading for the rest of their lives. So go ahead and get to it already!

. . .

Oh, you're still reading this book instead of dropping everything to go read to your child right this very second? Hm. Well, we guess that means you still have questions about this whole "when to read to your bookmonster" thing. Fair enough. Here are our answers to some frequently asked questions—feel free to read them whenever you want!

At what age should I start reading to my child?

It's never too early to start reading to your child. And we do mean *never*. Research shows that babies can react to and remember what has been read or sung to them before they're even born! You can try it out yourself the next time you happen to have a baby growing inside your belly. Just repeatedly read a favorite book to your future bookmonster starting around the third trimester. After the baby is born, lay the little one down for some storytime. After reading a new, unfamiliar book out loud, try reading the familiar, favorite one—and see how differently your baby reacts. Increased pacifier sucking, wilder kicks, or wider eyes might just tell you how much your newborn already remembers!

You might even feel the baby react while you're still pregnant. We had that incredible experience when Amber was preggo with our first child and would frequently feel her baby bump moving around while she read favorite books like *Guess How Much I Love You* by Sam McBratney out loud. And this cool little trick works with songs as well. Andy sang "Mrs. Train" by They Might Be Giants to our daughter in utero so often that he became able to manipulate test results at the OB/GYN's office—as soon as he'd belt out a few bars, the baby's heartbeat would go off the charts!

Because your child has been ready to listen to you from the very start, it's vital that you begin reading books as soon as possible. Try to avoid thinking of it as a future to-do item, like one of your New Year's resolutions—because we know what happens with those, don't we, Cobweb-Covered Treadmill in the Corner of the Basement? Activities that benefit your child's development aren't *should-dos*—they're *must-dos*.

At what age should I stop reading aloud to my child?

Never.

That's really the whole answer, but here's some more info for those of you who want to know why. People sometimes think that reading out loud is no longer necessary after kids start reading on their own. But shared reading teaches your child a bunch of lessons at different stages of literary development! These include:

1. **Prereading:** Children learn prerequisites for reading like realizing that books have fronts and backs, understanding that text is always read in the same direction, learning how to turn pages, identifying letters, and many other seemingly minor skills that form the foundation for reading.

2. **Initial reading:** Children develop skills in *phonological recoding* (the idea that letters are symbols that correspond to specific sounds we make while speaking) and also begin blending sounds together to read their first words.

3. **Confirmation fluency:** Children gain the ability to read in a controlled and automatic way, with competent speed, accuracy, and expression.

4. **Reading to learn new information:** Children become adept at using their newly acquired reading skills to learn other information, like science, social studies, and even math.

5. **Multiple viewpoints:** Typically, in the teenage years, children learn more complex uses of text, especially that text can be understood from multiple points of view. For example, children begin to appreciate that historical events would be conceived of very differently according to who is recounting the incident.

6. **Construction and reconstruction:** This stage continues indefinitely throughout adulthood as readers think more critically about text, build a detailed understanding of the types of materials they choose to read, and analyze writers' viewpoints against their own.

When you read aloud to your bookmonster, you can act as a guide through these book-related lessons. And when they read aloud to you, you'll be able to hear exactly how they're progressing.

This is particularly important to help kids avoid what educators describe as the dreaded "fourth grade reading slump." *(DUN DUN DUNNNNNNN!)* See, there's this thing that happens between the third and fourth grade, where students are expected to make the transition from learning to read, to reading to learn. Did you catch that subtle shift there? Up until fourth grade, one of the main lessons kids were being instructed in was how to read. But now they're supposed to have reading pretty much figured out. Teachers aren't going to spend time explaining that anymore. And pretty much every school subject—not just English—will require students to read increasingly sophisticated and unfamiliar words to understand what's going on in class. This can mean quickly declining grades for children lacking good, solid reading skills.

But here's the crazy thing. Fourth grade also happens to be a really common time for many parents to stop reading aloud to their children. Do you think it's a coincidence that a reading slump arrives right when you close the cover on your family's read-together routine? We don't think so. That's why it's a wonderful idea to keep reading aloud even after your child is already independently reading. It can help you identify any difficulties that might arise and enable you to continually help build your child's reading skills.

Is bedtime the best time for book reading?

We get why you might be wondering this. Tons of children's books these days end with the main character going to sleep. Books like *When We're Together* by Claire Freedman, *I Love You, Daddy* by Jillian Harker, *Bert & Ernie's First Book of Opposites* by Heather Au and enough other examples that we're pretty sure we could fill the rest of this book with their titles. Don't believe us? Check out the children's books lying around your house and you'll see exactly what we mean. We haven't actually performed the calculations, but we're fairly certain the Books That End with Sleep vs. Books Where Everyone Stays Awake ratio falls right around 97 to 1.

Plus there is research to support the idea that reading a book at bedtime has benefits. Experts have long recommended that parents use a consistent bedtime routine with children, which follows the same set of behaviors (like bathing, toothbrushing, singing, reading) in the same order night after night prior to bed. Families that do this fare better in multiple areas, including better sleep for kids (with more consistent sleep throughout the night and fewer instances of night waking) and better parental moods (obviously). Researchers further examined the importance of including a literacy element, like singing a song, reading a book, or telling a story as part the routine, and found that it was related to both better sleep for kids and higher language test scores.

So, while it is a good idea to include some kind of language activity before bed, it doesn't necessarily have to be book reading. One thing we like to do to mix things up is tell stories "from our minds," which tend to be either actual autobiographical memories from when we were kids, or totally fantastical, fictional tales. Sometimes we won't even say which type of story we're telling—and let the kids try to figure out whether we did, in fact, "fart our pants off" once when we were their age.

We understand that authors are writing so many books with sleepy endings in the hopes of helping parents put their kids to bed. But enough is enough. Modern parents are getting the idea that books are *only* for bedtime. And that's simply not the case. Limiting stories to bedtime can actually limit your child's literacy development. Because if you only read with your kid before going to sleep, then they could learn to associate reading with sleep (which would be disastrous for future school study sessions). Furthermore, they could end their habit of reading altogether when you eventually stop tucking them into bed at night.

Want to avoid these possible prose-related pitfalls? Then buck the modern trend of bedtime-centered reading, and make sure to share books and stories with your kid *all around the clock*. Some of our favorite times have included:

- During an excursion to the park—somewhere between running around and snacking and running around and snacking again.

- Right after a bath, when the kids are still cuddled up in a comfy towel, and not quite ready to do the whole pajamas-hairbrush-toothbrush rigmarole.

- In a doctor's office waiting room. Or absolutely any time you have to wait for anything, anywhere.

- At the coffee shop, because sitting down for a drink and book is an easy, fun outing for everyone.

- In the car, when you can listen to an audiobook instead of holding and reading a traditional one.

- In those sleepy minutes before breakfast when getting up doesn't sound attractive, but staying under the covers to share a book does.

- As a perfect excuse for absolutely any time you crave a cozy cuddle.

Try to incorporate book reading throughout the day, both spontaneously and at regularly scheduled times. But be flexible. Sometimes your normal time won't work, and that's OK. If you're devoted to reading together and creative about how you'll get it done, you'll surely be able to find many different ways and times to squeeze in some pages.

Since my kids have homework during the school year, can I skip reading out loud?

Spending time reading out loud is important year-round and can greatly benefit your child's ability to listen and learn in school. Think about it—at the same time your child is listening and talking with you about the book, they're simultaneously developing the following ferocious skills that will help them succeed in the classroom:

- listening
- concentrating
- sitting quietly
- comprehending auditory information
- understanding words and print

Because half the battle of doing schoolwork (or any other kind of work for that matter) is being able to quiet down, sit still, and use your brain for significant periods of time, the more practice your child gets at it the better. These benefits of reading are part of the reason that many elementary school teachers assign reading homework to begin with.

Continuing to read aloud together gives kids the opportunity to experience books differently than if they just read them by themselves. Sharing and discussing a book with others opens kids' eyes to aspects of the text they wouldn't have thought of on their own. (Just like you've experienced yourself if you've ever been part of a book club, or had a lively conversation with someone who's enjoyed the same book you have.) Reading aloud together turns an often-solitary act into a social activity, so it's an amazing springboard for conversations and bonding. When people talk about spending "quality time" with kids, read-aloud time definitely qualifies!

The Reading Promise: My Father and the Books We Shared by Alice Ozma recounts a pretty amazing story about how a fourth grader and her dad made a goal to read aloud together for a hundred consecutive days. But they ended up loving it so much that they continued their daily reading streak all the way up until she left for college. This father–daughter pair made so many sweet memories reading together that she actually wrote a book about it. Can you imagine how awesome it would be to send your precious little one away to college with a whole dorm full of positive memories from the time you spent hanging out together?

Since summer break is all about relaxing, can I skip the reading then?

By now we're sure you have some idea about how we're going to answer this, but here goes anyway . . .

NO.

Summertime is actually the most important time of the year to read. For decades, researchers have known about something called the "summer reading setback" or "summer learning effect," which describes a common seasonal pattern of children's reading progress. According to this effect, students of all reading levels tend to make significant gains during the school year, but then dramatic differences emerge between children with higher and lower reading scores over the summer. Kids who already have better literacy skills tend to continue their good progress, gaining reading knowledge and potential for standardized test points even when school is not in session. But kids who have worse literacy skills tend to stagnate and fail to gain any reading points over the summer at all.

In lay-monster terms, that means that bookmonsters continue gobbling up books and gaining roarsome skills over the summer, leaving their ordinary human friends falling further and further behind. What you do at home to encourage your child to love books and practice reading is massively important—*especially* when school is out.

How long should I spend reading each day?

There's no magic number for how many minutes you need to spend reading to your child each day. And when you commit to having fun with books and reading, you'll find that it naturally varies over time. Some days you'll want to dive into books and spend the entire afternoon reading, and other days you'll just squeeze a story in here and there.

We suggest that you set your goal by fun instead of by the clock. Just try to keep reading in chunks that you and your child can handle. And please, please, please, we're begging you—never set a timer for your reading sessions. We've heard this recommendation before, and it's nearly made us scream. By setting a timer, you're essentially training your child to think of reading as a chore, and the timer bell as the long-awaited sound of sweet freedom. Since the key to lasting literacy is to make your kid love to read, this is the absolute wrong way to go about it. Don't set a timer, bribe kids with sticker charts and other rewards, or do anything else that's going to make the act of reading itself feel less fun.

Just commit to making reading a regular—and joyful—part of every, single day. No matter when or how long you do it.

6

The Right Way to Read to a Bookmonster

When a lion tamer does his job correctly, audiences "ooh" and "ahh." When he does it incorrectly, they say, "Ewwwww, that's a lot of blood" and "Aaaaaahhhhh, run for your lives because that lion we previously thought was tame is actually wild and loose and coming right for us!"

The job of reading to a bookmonster isn't nearly as dangerous as all that. But it's just as important to make sure you're doing it the right way.

How can that be, you may ask? It's not like reading a book is a life or death situation, right? While it's true that no one will get their head bitten off by the king of the jungle just because you stink at storytime, too many poor reading performances might just kill off your kid's love of books. And that's a tragedy that lasts a lifetime.

To make sure that doesn't happen, let's first make sure we can identify the *wrong* way to read to kids. And yes, when your goal is to instill a lifelong love of reading in your child, there *is* a wrong way. Even if you and your child sat down with a floor-to-ceiling stack of the best books ever written, and you read every single word on every single page every single day, you wouldn't automatically be on the road to raising a bookmonster. Research confirms that it takes more than just reading often to improve your child's literacy skills. *How* you read is at least as important as *what* and *how often* you read.

So please, for goodness' sake, don't try to make reading to your kid quick and efficient, as if you were reading an email, a news article or—the horror!—a software update user agreement. Successfully getting children immersed in books requires much more than simply reciting the words, one page after another without stopping. To get them to truly hear, see, and feel the entire story, you often need to talk about more than what's been written. And you need to let your kid do some talking, too.

Reading is a conversation

The biggest mistake many adults make when reading to kids? Thinking they have to do all the talking. Sure, since you're probably the only person in the room who actually knows how to read already, it's your job to make sure all the words on the page get read. But children benefit most when you help them go beyond the text itself—connecting stories to experiences they've had in their lives, teaching them unfamiliar concepts, explaining difficult passages, and encouraging them to form their own thoughts and feelings about what you're reading. The only way all those amazing things can happen is if you stop reading every once in a while and start chatting with your bookmonster instead!

That's why we say that shared book reading should be less of a lecture, and more of a conversation. If you ever feel like you're delivering a monologue, figure out how to turn it into a dialogue. Or to put it another way: You need to read *with* your kid, not *to* your kid. When you master this one simple strategy, book reading becomes not only more educational, but also way more fun.

When she was two and a half, our littlest daughter showed us how much she already understood this lesson. One of her favorite books was *Brown Bear, Brown Bear, What Do You See?* by Bill Martin Jr. and Eric Carle. After we had read the book enough times for her to have it completely memorized, she decided that she would "read it" to us. She proudly flipped through the pages, sure enough reciting the whole darn thing word-for-word. That is, until she got to the part about the "white dog looking at me"—at which point she paused briefly to talk about how "in our home, we do have a cat but we don't have a dog"—before moving on to faithfully recite the rest of the book as written. Even at this young age, she understood that books can be better when you stop to discuss them. Rest assured, if our toddler could get the hang of turning book reading into a conversation, then so can you!

One incredibly cool thing about approaching reading this way is that it allows you and your child to learn together. While they'll receive lessons in spelling, grammar, vocabulary, and the content of the books you're reading, you'll get to find out more about what they're interested in and the unique ways they think. Reading to our own kids has allowed us to discover that our oldest daughter loves being adventurous, so she often chooses books about magic, travel, and kids doing important, grown-up things. It's probably also why she enjoys the challenge of reading big, long books filled with beyond-her-grade-level vocabulary words. Our middle son is a huge fan of wordplay, like rhymes, made-up words, and unusual verse. That's why he was such a big fan of *The BFG* by Roald Dahl—he just couldn't get enough of the giant's funny sayings and idiosyncratic speech. And our youngest daughter loves repetition of her favorite stories. In a house full of books, she has us read the same handful over and over (so it's no wonder she was already memorizing them at age two).

Learning all about your child while you bond over a book will serve you in many ways. For one, it will make reading more fun for both of you, so it never feels like a chore. You'll also be better able to choose stories that match your kid's interests, which will help build excitement about future books you read together. And it's a great way to get to know each other better—sharing thoughts, coming up with inside jokes you'll crack up over later, and making memories that can last forever.

Check out this list of conversation starters that will help you and your child get the most out of each book. Keep them in mind as you read, and bring up whichever ones seem most relevant to the story or interesting to you and your child. The general themes here are appropriate to discuss with kids of all ages and reading levels, but you may want to tailor them to your child's level of understanding and individual interests. Use any or all of them in any combination you like, and be sure to always follow where the fun takes you!

Point at pictures

If the book you're reading has illustrations in it, there's automatically a lot for a kid to look at and enjoy. Make sure you give your little one plenty of time to examine all the details they want to before turning to the next page. This is especially relevant when reading picture books that contain no or relatively few words, like the enchanting, dance-filled *Flora and the Flamingo* by Molly Idle and the illustration-rich My Big Wimmelbooks series published by The Experiment. To help your kid make connections between the book's pictures and words, point frequently to the illustrations that match the text you're reading. For example:

- "Do you like green eggs and ham?" (while pointing to the green eggs and ham)
- "A little egg lay on a leaf" (while pointing to the abstractly painted white dot that your kiddo might not have known was supposed to be an egg, and which will soon turn into a very hungry caterpillar)
- "Where's Waldo?" (while pointing to hundreds of people all dressed just like Waldo)

Point at words

Pointing at words and letters while you read them instantly communicates to even tiny tykes that there's something very special about those otherwise unintelligible squiggles and shapes. Point to the title on the cover when you first sit down and say the name of the book you're about to read together. Later, let your finger follow along some lines of text as you speak. And if a character ever happens to shout something in the story, try pointing *extra hard* at *each word* for *emphasis*!

You can also discuss letters more explicitly by pointing them out and talking about the sounds they make. This is easiest (and often most fun!) when the words are actually pictured in the illustrations. Like if you notice that there are several drawings of a jar with "JAM" written on its side in *Bread and Jam for Frances* by Russell Hoban, you could point to the jar and ask your child what it might say. Whether your child is right or wrong, you can spend time reinforcing that you can tell it says "jam" because the *J* says "juh," the *A* says "aaa," and the *M* says "mmm." Then say the juh-aaa-mmm sounds closer and closer together until you're saying the word "jam." If you want, you can continue the conversation by asking if they know any words that rhyme with jam, or that start with *J*, or any other letter-related questions that come to mind.

Whenever you see words duplicated on a page, like in the title of *Busy, Busy Town* by Richard Scarry, point it out. Research shows that comparison is a particularly effective way for kids to learn, and comparing two examples of the same word can help kids realize that the arrangement of letters is an important clue to knowing what the word says.

More questions you might want to ask:

- This word says "dog." Can you find another word on the page that also says "dog"?
- "Family" starts with *F*. Can you think of another word that starts with *F*?
- How are the words "happy" and "hungry" alike?

Explain new words and unfamiliar content

Learning new words is important to bookmonsters all throughout life. It helps them amass large early vocabularies that make learning to read easier, it leads to success on the vocabulary section of the SAT, and it gives them more creative things to yell when cars cut them off during rush hour.

Kids will naturally learn lots of new words from reading books with you, and the older they get, the better they'll be at using context clues to deduce an unfamiliar word's meaning. But you can be a big help by explicitly defining new words for your kid. When you encounter a word that you know your child is unfamiliar with, or one that stands out as particularly interesting, take a second to explain what it means or guide your child through figuring it out.

The same goes for unfamiliar situations or sayings. Children's books are loaded with circumstances your child has never been in (like when the princess in *Little Miss Princess* by Roger Hargreaves has to go to separate butcher, baker, and greengrocer shops to buy food) and sayings they've never heard (like confusion over "drawing the drapes" in *Amelia Bedelia* by Peggy Parish). As you're reading, try to look at the book from your child's perspective—think about what they might be confused about, and talk about it. Possible comments could include:

- That's an interesting word. Can you figure out what it means from the sentence?
- Check it out! A baby goat is called a kid, just like you!
- Have you ever heard of the Alamo before? It's a big, old fort in Texas where a famous battle took place a long time ago. Remember it.

Don't worry that stopping might ruin your momentum or make the story boring—it will actually help to enhance your child's comprehension and enjoyment of the text. When our oldest bookmonster was in third grade, Amber was reading *The Naughtiest Girl Marches On* by Anne Digby with her and paused to explain what the word "accommodate" means. Several pages later, our daughter looked up, smiled, and thanked Mom for taking the time to explain words to her. Pretty cool, right? Kids really do appreciate the efforts we make to help them understand stories better!

Teach some specifics

Do you have any particular lessons you'd like your kid to learn? Whether it's shapes, colors, counting, rhyming, or metaphors, books are ideal places to find lots of examples to discuss. In fact, many children's books are built for this exact purpose.

When teaching something new, always try to push the conversation just a bit beyond what your child already knows. Reading often will help you do this, because your frequent conversations will give you a pretty good idea of what your little one understands. Here are some sample questions:

- Can you find a square in the picture?
- So there were ten butterflies before, but now that one flew away, how many are left?
- Do you think the author meant that the character was an *actual* peach? Let's try to think of more metaphors like that one.

Ask questions like it's your job

Pretend you're a professional news reporter, and ask the famous "Five W" questions: Who, What, When, Where, and Why (and you might as well throw in How while you're at it). These questions help journalists tell complete stories in their writing, and because they're open-ended and can't be answered with a simple yes or no, they're also perfect for getting your bookmonster gabbing. Try:

- Who was your favorite character?
- What surprised you most about the story?
- When did you first suspect who the culprit was?
- Where did the story take place?
- Why do you think the character did that?
- How did the character know that?

Continue the conversation by asking for more information from your child, or sharing your own perspective on things. Of course the littlest bookmonsters won't have the verbal skills required to engage in complex back-and-forth conversation, and that's totally OK. Initially you'll be doing most of the talking, and your child will add more and more to the discussion before you know it.

Get inside characters' heads

As an adult, you're an expert at reading between the lines to comprehend a story, but it takes several years and lots of practice with literature for a bookmonster to build up those skills. So many aspects of books that may be obvious to you—like the feelings and motivations of characters—might go completely unnoticed by your bookmonster.

Look at some children's books, and you'll find that the words don't always tell the whole story. You have to make inferences about how characters are thinking to actually understand why they behave the way they do. For example, *Noisy Nora* by Rosemary Wells features a family of mice. Throughout the book, Father plays with the oldest child, Mother cares for the baby, and the middle daughter, Nora, makes lots and lots of noise. Savvy adult readers like you can identify why Nora is so noisy—she wants attention, of course! But absolutely nowhere in the book does it *say* that. So whenever you read, try to notice how much information is *not* included in the text and might be going unappreciated by your budding bookmonster. Then start a conversation about it, with questions like:

- How do you think the character feels?
- Would you feel happy or sad if that happened to you?
- What does the character want, and why can't they have it?

Get inside characters' faces

Books are full of words that describe fun facial expressions and gestures, like shrug, gasp, grimace, grin, nod . . . and on and on. When you encounter them in a story, try acting them out with your kid! Doing so is helpful for lots of reasons. First, it's just plain entertaining. Really. We can't think of a better way to bring more drama, expression, and giggly fun to reading together. Second, it helps kids understand what the words mean when they encounter them in the future. Finally, acting out facial expressions and gestures can support your child's ability to understand what is happening in the story and empathize with characters. Amber is a full-grown adult, and she often finds herself shrugging, grimacing, or otherwise acting in sync with characters in novels she's reading even now. And you know what? It's *still* helpful for understanding the story! Some questions to try out:

- Do you remember what "curtsy" means?
- Ooh, that character is grinning—does that mean she's happy or sad?
- Can you show me your best disgusted face? (Also, please stop using that face at the dinner table.)

Get emotional

Remember that books are entertainment for kids. If you want them to enjoy reading as much as all the action-packed video screens competing for their attention out there, you've got to put on quite a show. So go nuts:

- Read with expression.
- Milk dramatic pauses to capture moments of suspense.
- Try using different voices for the characters.

And do all that stuff right now, when your kid is too young to realize just how *so totally embarrassing* you are.

Converse about story construction

It doesn't matter if it's a children's book, a major motion picture, or coworker gossip by the water cooler—good stories always have the same essential elements: setting, characters, plot, conflict, and resolution. Understanding these elements will help your kid comprehend books, get decent grades in English, and learn how to tell their own stories. You can practice by discussing the parts of the stories you read together:

- How would the story be different if it was set somewhere else?
- Do the characters remind you of anyone you know?
- Stories usually have a big problem. What's the problem in this one?
- How do you think the characters are going to resolve the problem? Let's keep reading and see if you're right!

Consider a story's lesson

Most children's stories contain a lesson or moral, but it may not be immediately obvious to your child. Discussing what each of you think the lesson might be and how you might apply it to your lives can really boost kids' comprehension. Ask:

- What do you think the moral of the story was?
- Have you ever experienced a problem like the one we read about?
- How do you think you could use this lesson in your own life?

Discuss family values

Not all book characters are nice, and sometimes they do some naughty things. Even when the story has a great lesson, you often have to read about a lot of bad behavior before getting to it. For example, *The Berenstain Bears No Girls Allowed* by Stan and Jan Berenstain ultimately results in everybody playing together, but you have to read through some grating gender stereotyping and exclusion to find it.

Keep in mind that kids don't learn just from the feel-good resolution of the book—they can also pick up on the undesirable stuff, too. So instead of ignoring bad behavior when you read about it, use it to reinforce your family's values and expectations. Have open conversations about whether you agree with what the characters did and how you might do it differently by asking:

- Do you think these characters handled the situation well? Or, what should they have done instead?
- Oooh, hitting is not OK, is it?
- If you were the character, how would you have tried to solve the problem?

Relate the story to your own life

No matter what you're learning, you always remember it better if it relates to your own experience. Help your kid get more from stories by relating them to things you've done in real life—or create new real-life experiences inspired by what you read! Sample questions:

- The characters are at the zoo. What do you remember from when you went to the zoo?

- This story takes place in Antarctica. Can you help me find it on the globe?

- That book made skiing sound like fun. Should we try skiing sometime soon?

Let your child fill in the blanks

Here's a simple way to get your kid more engaged in the story: let them read some of it! After your little sponge has heard a book a few times, there's a good chance they have some of it memorized. Test it out by reading everything but the last part of a sentence, like "one fish, two fish, red fish . . ."

. . . Has your kid said "blue fish" yet?

Another fun fill-in-the-blank strategy is to ask children what they think will happen next. It doesn't matter if it's a mundane prediction or a totally wild one. For example, in *Iggy Peck, Architect* by Andrea Beaty, you might guess that Iggy would build a bridge to save them from being stranded on the island. But what if he rigged up a cable-propelled gondola instead? Both possibilities could be really entertaining to discuss. Use your imaginations and have some fun with it, with questions like:

- What do you think will happen next?
- Do you think the character is going to get in trouble?
- How do you think the story will end?

Fill in the blanks *incorrectly*

When you're raising bookmonsters, you'll be asked to read out loud a lot. So if you find yourself getting bored by reading the same books over and over, try mixing it up by reading the wrong words every once in a while. Andy loves doing this with books the kids know well, sometimes saying the wrong title multiple times before getting it right, like:

- "The Cat in the Dress" (Kids: "No!")
- "The Dog in the Hat" (Kids: "Noooo!")
- "The Moose in the Three-Piece Suit" (Kids: "Noooooooooo!")
- "Oh, I see. The Cat in the Hat." (Kids: "Good. Now read.")

You can try it on the title, or anyplace in the book when you want to rile up your kid and entertain yourself at the same time.

Share your reactions to the story

An obvious but powerful way to discuss a book with your child is to simply say what you liked about it. Everybody loves doing this—that's why adults join book clubs, right? (Well, maybe having a couple hours with zero kids and a nice bottle of rosé has something to do with it, too.)

But the fact remains that books are fun to talk about. So next time you share a story, pour your little reading partner a glass of white (milk), and share your thoughts on these questions:

- What was your favorite part of the book?
- Would you change anything?
- How did you feel about the ending?

If you're wondering how much talking versus reading you should be doing, that's something you'll have to feel out on a book-by-book basis. There's no particular formula to follow, and some books will have you pausing to gab more than others. As you read, gauge your child's level of interest, and stop to talk when you notice anything that seems particularly curious, important, or eye-catching to either of you. A good clue as to whether you should stop reading to talk or stop talking to get back to reading is how good a time you're having. If things start to feel stale, try tweaking your read-to-talk ratio a bit. It will get easier and easier as incorporating conversation into your reading becomes more natural.

Just keep in mind that at all times and no matter what, book reading should be about fun. The more fun it is, the more likely you'll do it frequently. And frequent readers become ferocious bookmonsters!

Reading to Multiple Bookmonsters at Once

In our house, we often find ourselves reading to more than one bookmonster at the same time. If you feel intimidated at the very thought of this, don't be! You can use all the conversation starters from this chapter whether you're reading to a single child or a classroom full of kids.

When reading to children of varying ages, you'll want to keep their diverse levels of comprehension in mind so that everyone can take part in the conversation. Ask little ones if they understand what's happening during particularly difficult passages, and allow older ones to help provide the recaps if they want. If a potentially unfamiliar word pops up, ask the kids if they know what it means, starting with the youngest child first so that everyone gets a chance to answer. Our kids love to guess what particularly big words mean before we explain their definitions—it's a great way for older bookmonsters to challenge themselves, and it also keeps younger ones up to speed on the plot.

A bigger reading group can also be a fun excuse to let book-reading get a little raucous. In *The Lion and the Little Red Bird* by Elisa Kleven, the lion paints vivid pictures on a cave wall using his tail as a paintbrush while the little red bird looks on. Invite your bunch of bookmonsters to interact with the story by calling out their favorite colors or doing their best impersonation of each character.

Don't worry about having to plan conversations or age adjustments ahead of time. When you remember to approach reading with multiple bookmonsters as a fun opportunity for interaction and group bonding, these things will likely come naturally. Just remember to include everybody, and give kids the space to converse with each other as well as with you.

PART II

Making Your Bookmonster Feel at Home

When you have babies, you fill your house with gear like cribs, diapers, electrical outlet plug covers, and soft swaddling blankets. When you have bookmonsters, you stock up on all the things that make them feel comfortable, too. That's what the next several chapters are all about—showing you how to create the ideal environment for your bookmonster to grow and flourish. We'll cover strategies for doing this both at home and out and about, whether your kid is alone or with friends, and even when toys and screens are competing for their attention. By weaving language and literacy activities into children's lives and surroundings in a natural, fun-loving way, bookmonsters end up living, loving, and learning all at the same time—all day long.

7

Setting a Bookmonster Trap

Mice go for cheese. Raccoons go for marshmallows. And sheep go wherever some dude holding a big curved stick decides to send them. The bookmonster hiding inside your child is attracted to certain types of bait as well. By filling your surroundings with as many of the following tempting tools as possible, you'll be able to lure out and capture that cute little creature before you know it!

Books

Since your goal is to raise your kid as a bookmonster, you'll obviously want to keep your home stocked with plenty of books to read. But don't make the mistake of putting them all in one place. Instead, spread your books out and store them in multiple locations, especially those your child visits or passes by often:

- on a shelf in your child's bedroom
- alongside toy bins in the playroom
- filling a cupboard in the hallway
- in a basket in the family room
- by the potty in the bathroom

And anyplace else that makes sense for your kiddo. When you place easily seen, easily accessed reading material all along your bookmonster's typical "migration routes," they're bound to take the bait and start flipping through pages sooner or later.

Words for reading

For kids developing early literacy skills, any reading is good reading. So make sure there are plenty of letters and words for your child to see and think about, both inside and outside of books. Some easy examples to add to your collection include:

- letter blocks to build and spell with
- alphabet puzzles to develop spatial skills while learning letters
- ABC magnets to stick all over the fridge
- labeled bins for things like toy animals, beads, and train tracks, to keep your family organized

- word-filled artwork to inspire you (We have a painting of a bicycle that says "Life is a beautiful ride" in our living room, but if "Mama needs some wine" is more your style, we say go for it!)

Materials for writing

Bookmonsters like creating text as much as they enjoy consuming it. So keep plenty of supplies handy for whenever inspiration strikes. Fill a kid's art corner with pens, pencils, crayons, markers—and of course, loads and loads of paper. Easels with whiteboards on them are perfect for playing school and for writing and rewriting as much as they want. And if you're feeling crafty, you can even buy special paint to turn a wall of your choice into a real, working chalkboard! (Just make sure your kid understands they're only allowed to write on this *one* wall, not *all* of them!)

Role models

Here's one more item no bookmonster can resist: *You!* Remember that the example you set has an immense influence on your little one. Be sure to have numerous conversations so your kid hears a rich and varied vocabulary. Read books to your child often so reading becomes a fun source of entertainment. And let them see you reading grown-up books on your own, too, so they know that reading will always be an important part of life . . . even when they get super-duper old like you!

8

A Bookmonster's Natural Habitat

From snow fleas high atop the Himalayas to snailfish beneath the ocean's darkest depths, all living organisms seek specific environments that suit them best. Bookmonsters, too, have ideal surroundings where they go to find comfort, quiet, and plenty of reading material to feast on. What is this wondrous place where your growing bookmonster can thrive and flourish? The library, of course!

Filled with stacks of books to sit among and countless stories to explore, libraries are custom-made to bring a love of reading out of any kid (or adult) who encounters them. But libraries come in more shapes and sizes than you may realize. Here is some helpful info about three distinct styles of libraries your bookmonster will surely want to see!

The public library

Once bookmonsters have acquired a taste for reading, their appetite for more and more pages to devour will truly become insatiable. That's why the public library is so perfect—no matter how many books your kid goes through, the library always has *more*!

So don't be surprised when the local library becomes one of your child's absolute favorite outings.

Our own kids have been longtime library fans, yet they still blew us away when they started choosing it as their top destination for many of their most special days. Like when the new school year was rapidly approaching and we asked our firstborn daughter if there was anything she wanted to try to squeeze in before summer ended. Mind you, we'd done some pretty cool stuff over the past months, like swimming at the pool, playing at the beach, riding the train to the museum, and going on hikes and bike rides. Yet instead of asking to repeat any of those exciting excursions, she earnestly answered, "There is one thing I'd really like to do . . . I'd like to go to the library." We smiled at her utter adorableness and said, "OK, we'll take you there *again*." Months later when our son's birthday rolled around, we had a party planned for the weekend, but a free weekday on his actual birthday. Again, we offered that he could choose whatever he wanted to do for his special day, and his one request was to go to the library.

Before you dismiss our kids as the super-nerdy-offspring-of-a-couple-of-dorky-parents, consider why it is that our kids enjoy reading stories so much. Remember that their love of reading stems from the joyful memories they've made curling up with us to read together. By sharing stories with our children, we've associated books with cuddles, conversations, laughter, and love. And when you think about it like that, going to the library to pick out new stories to read together suddenly sounds pretty attractive to us parents, too.

When you're bringing up bookmonsters, we recommend that you embrace your local library immediately. Get your brood over there as soon as possible, get yourself a library card, and get used to the scenery—because you're going to be there a lot! Here are a few of our top tips for making the most of your visits:

Explore the possibilities

The children's section of the library contains many different types of books, including board books, picture books, chapter books, graphic novels, nonfiction, audiobooks, poetry, mysteries, and more. Empower your kid to try out new genres and styles by frequently looking through these sections together.

Let kids take the lead

Try not to confine your child to books of any particular topic, level, or type. Instead, let them follow their interests and pick out whatever they want. Sure, you'll head home with books that you may not have chosen yourself, but you'll also end up with a really excited kiddo. And the more captivated kids are by the books they check out, the more likely they will be to read them.

But go ahead and make some "parent picks," too

Remember your favorite books and authors from back when you were a kid? Share them with your little one now and you'll get to enjoy them all over again! Amber has loved introducing our little ones to fantastical Roald Dahl classics like *James and the Giant Peach* and *The Witches*, while Andy digs cracking them up with the hilarious weirdness of Daniel Pinkwater tales like *The Hoboken Chicken Emergency* and *The Snarkout Boys and the Avocado of Death*.

Try the library search engine

Show your kid how easy it is to look up books using the online library catalog. Kids can help type in search terms and will be excited to see all the results that pop up. Search for specific book titles, additional books by authors they've enjoyed, or your child's favorite topics. You can narrow your search to show only books that are available at the branch you're currently visiting (a very handy feature in case your library system has lots of different locations like ours does). Seeing books first on the computer screen and then physically materializing on the shelf can be really fun for kids—and it reinforces the notion that libraries are marvelously magical places!

Ask your librarian for help

Librarians are absolute experts on accessing library resources, so don't be afraid to ask them to lend you a hand. When our daughter went through a protracted phase of being completely obsessed with doctors, we thought we'd read every book at our library on the topic— but our librarian surprised us by scrounging up even more. And every time we potty trained any of our kids, we always began by heading to the info desk and asking our librarians for as many potty-related books, videos, and CDs as they could find. The *piles* they *plopped* in front of us had us *flush* with reading material faster than we could count to *number two*!

Bring reusable tote bags

We've never known a bookmonster to check out just one book, so you'll definitely want to bring a bag to carry all of their selections. And make sure it has strong, sturdy handles—children's books may seem small, but a bag full of them sure is heavy!

Read some of your selections immediately

Help limit the number of books you lug away with you by sorting your kiddo's selections into two separate piles: one stack to check out and take home, and another one to read immediately and leave at the library. Kids love the instant gratification of being able to read together right then and there!

Return books directly to the librarian

We know it's fun to listen to your books go *thunk, thunk, thunk* as you drop them into the library's big book return drop box—so definitely do that with your kid from time to time—but on days when you intend to return oodles of old books before checking out a big batch of brand-new ones, you may want to skip the slot. That's because if the librarian doesn't fish your old books out of the return bin before you're ready to leave with your new selections, the computer system may think you have too many books checked out at once, and say you're over your checkout limit. To skip this potential A-B-C-Disaster, simply hand your returns directly to the librarians when you walk in. When you explain that your bookmonster is raring to borrow more books, they'll be happy to help!

Get the kids their own library cards

Sometimes signing up for additional accounts is more hassle than it's worth. Like when you apply for a store credit card to get 10 percent off some new throw pillows, and suddenly you have a whole slew of separate bills and due dates to keep track of. (Also, the kids are going to destroy those pillows in, like, five minutes anyway.) But children's library cards are an extra account you should totally go for. Because your family will have more than one account to use, you'll be able to check out more books at once. They also some-times come with unexpected benefits, like *no late fees* for overdue books on kids' accounts. And most important, being able to wield their very own library card will bring a look of unmistakable pride to your child's face. And that's priceless!

Enjoy your quiet afternoon

Once a couple of our kids became big enough to read on their own, we realized that a major benefit of going to the library is the quiet hours it gives us afterward. The house is never more peaceful than when it contains hundreds of crisp, new pages to completely cap-tivate your kid's attention. So sit back, relax, and maybe even curl up with some reading material of your own!

Sign up for a summer reading program

Many libraries offer free incentives to keep children reading over summer break. Kids will enjoy keeping track of the hours they spend reading, and then racking up rewards like toys, restaurant coupons, and books they get to keep. And you'll enjoy the cleverly disguised preparation it provides for the upcoming school year.

Check out the unique special events your local library offers

Today's libraries often go well beyond traditional storytime fare to offer loads of other special programs and events. Here are a few faves our kids have gotten to experience: painting on canvas, LEGO building, an educational drum demonstration and raucous jam session (yes, *in a library*), Mother's and Father's Day crafts, movie screenings, author talks, and magic shows. There was even a teddy bear sleepover where our pajama-clad kids read to their stuffed animals before leaving them to stay overnight at the library, and then came back the next morning to find them holding tiny albums full of pictures showing the stuffed animals having a tea party, watching a movie, sleeping in tiny sleeping bags, and doing all the other stuff they supposedly did during their slumber party. We know, we have an awesome library. But so do you. Go check it out!

Keep Trying

If your trips to the library haven't yet been as magical as the ones we describe, try not to get discouraged. For months and months, our son was never interested when we offered to take him to storytime at the library. We figured it just wasn't his thing, and so we didn't go. Then one day his friend asked him on a storytime playdate. It happened to be at a different library branch led by a different librarian, and lo and behold— our son absolutely loved it. After all those months of missed library opportunities, it turned out he just wasn't crazy about the particular librarian who led the first storytimes he went to. Now that he realized there were other people out there willing to read in silly voices and hold up the pictures for him, he was all about it! So whatever your bookmonster's particular library-related obstacle is, there's probably a way around it. You just need to find it!

The home library

Your kid would probably love it if they could live at the public library 24-7. You might love it too, but unfortunately you are legally obligated to take them home with you at closing time. But that's OK, especially if you keep all that literary love going with a big, beautiful collection of books at home.

Studies in numerous countries around the world have shown that no matter where children live or what language they speak, having a substantial number of books in the home is important for gaining great reading skills. In these studies, researchers counted how many books were in each child's home and compared that number to the same child's fourth grade reading score. In every culture, a consistent pattern held true: children whose homes contained lots of books (about 100 or more) stood out as better readers.

Here's why having plenty of books on hand is so important:

You can share them

Having books at the ready means that you'll be more likely to use them together as a family. And the more time you spend bonding over books, the better your bookmonster's skills can be!

Your kid can explore them independently

When you leave books out for your child to discover and explore, there's a good chance they will soon top their list of favorite toys. Be sure to make them easily available—don't store them too high up, in a closed closet, or in any other location that your bookmonster can't access quickly and frequently.

They show everyone that reading is a core family value

Having books on display is a loud and clear signal that books and reading are important to your family. Since your kid is crazy about you, participating in your book-loving family culture will be a source of pride.

When we told you about the importance of having at least 100 books at home, did you picture a tiny, kid-sized bookshelf full of children's storybooks? That would make sense, right? Well here's the interesting thing: it doesn't matter what kind of books they are. Researchers found that kids' reading scores were higher with *any* 100 books in the house—regardless of book type, length, or intended audience age. In fact, variety is an ideal ingredient to shoot for in your home library. Children benefit the most when they're exposed to a diverse array of books that cover different topics and represent various levels of difficulty. Having a wide assortment of selections in a home library helps ensure that children are always able to find something that interests them and matches their current and ever-advancing reading skills. Plus, lots of books for lots of reading levels means that each and every member of the family can enjoy them!

Don't forget to have some books on hand for yourself—and remember to use them! Let your child see you use a cookbook to make a recipe, read a user's manual to help you fix the vacuum cleaner, or simply spend time reading books for fun.

Consider the clear and damaging message you could be sending if you don't. If you only had children's books in the house and never modeled reading yourself, your child would come to believe that reading is only for little kids. And since children often want to do grown-up things as soon as possible, they would soon be clamoring to ditch their books in favor of whatever they perceive to be more adultlike stuff they see you doing instead. So make sure you collect as many books as you can, and crack them open often!

The Little Free Library

You may have heard about Little Free Libraries. Or you may have seen one, even if you didn't know what it was. Little Free Libraries are typically little wooden boxes with little roofs and little doors that people fill with books and put in front of their houses, apartment buildings, or businesses. They're kind of like birdfeeders for people hungry for books. And they might just be the perfect intersection between a public library and an at-home one.

The idea is that anyone from the community can come by and borrow a book—or leave a book—any time they like. Because the libraries are completely free to use, they're a great way to make more books available to people who may not have access to them, which is basically the mission of Little Free Library, the nonprofit organization that runs the program. You can check out their website at littlefreelibrary.org to find a massive map showing where community libraries are located, or to get information about starting one of your own. There are start-up costs involved in purchasing a premade box, or you can build one yourself and pay a much smaller fee to get registered on their map. Some people get super creative and repurpose used furniture or even appliances to house their libraries. Whether you end up creating your own Little Free Library or exploring the city to find one that already exists, your little bookmonster will get a big kick out of seeing how books bring communities together.

9

Bookmonsters
on the Loose

Birds fly south to survive the winter. Salmon swim upstream to lay their eggs. And elephants migrate seasonally to search for food. Bookmonsters leave home a lot, too—to tag along on errands, play at the park, attend a class, eat in a restaurant, go to the movies, and all sorts of other fun stuff. They don't face nearly the same dangers on their journeys as those other animals do (unless you forget to latch in their car seats and then take all your turns way too fast). But you still might think that once they set foot outside their natural, book-filled habitat, there will be no way for them to keep exercising their reading muscles.

Think again.

Road signs. Billboards. Bumper stickers. Store windows. Product labels. Price tags. Restaurant menus. Posters. Cash registers. Even public restroom wall graffiti. Once you open your eyes and start looking for it, you'll realize that *tons* of printed words exist outside your home—and each one you find represents an exciting opportunity for your bookmonster to learn. All you have to do is start a conversation about it.

Why is it a good idea to talk to your child about words you see in places other than books? One answer is that it gives your child extra practice reading, which can obviously help their skills improve. But there's another reason, too, and this one might surprise you: The more places you teach your kid about reading, the faster they will learn to do it.

Sounds a bit strange, huh? But so does jazz, and people listen to that all the time. See, it turns out that how well you learn something depends not only on *what* and *how* you study but also on *where* you study it. Numerous research scientists have figured out that there's a connection between test scores and test location. Specifically, people perform better when they are tested in the same place where they learned. So if your Intro to Economics seminar met in Auditorium 202 all semester long, but then your final exam was in Auditorium 303, congratulations! You can finally give your parents an excuse for why you ended up majoring in ceramics.

Children appear to be even more sensitive than adults when it comes to learning environment. One study involved teaching kids the names of a bunch of made-up objects sitting on a table. All the children learned and were tested in the same room, but when half of them were tested, there was a different tablecloth covering the table. The results showed that kids performed significantly better when they were tested on the same tablecloth that was there when they learned!

The reason why this happens is pretty interesting (if you're interested in that sort of thing). We experience all our senses simultaneously, so when we hear a professor talking about supply and demand, or a researcher telling us the name of a weird fuzzball thing on the table, we can't separate that auditory experience from the other sensations we're having at the same time—like smelling the unique aroma of this particular classroom or seeing what the tablecloth underneath that fuzzball looks like. And when test time comes, being in that same place and smelling or seeing the same things can provide additional cues that will help you remember what you learned.

What does all this mean for little bookmonsters like yours? That only teaching them about letters on the same old alphabet puzzle at home day in and day out just isn't going to cut it. Sure, they'll rock their ABCs when you discuss them using that particular puzzle, but if you want them to extend what they know to new and different-looking letters in new and different-looking situations, you need to let them learn in a mixture of familiar and unusual environments. That means helping your bookmonster find words and letters everywhere you go!

Driving in the car

Your kid might not believe it, but there was a time when screens were too big to leave the house, so children actually had to entertain themselves in the car. Fortunately, it's easy to bring those good old days back, and give your kid some valuable literacy lessons at the same time!

Play language games

There are miles and miles of fun games your family can choose from. Here are three of our family's favorites:

1. **The Alphabet Game:** Have everyone look out their windows at the road signs, cars, and license plates you pass and try to find each letter of the alphabet in order, from ALBUQUERQUE to ZEBRA CROSSING. This classic game is perfect for long road trips, but even short rides can be good for finding a few letters—just tell your kid to remember where they left off in the alphabet when you park, then start from there when you get back in the car.

2. **I Spy & Spell:** Normally when you play I Spy, you try to get people to guess a nearby object by telling them what color it is, as in, "I spy with my little eye something blue." To make the game more bookmonster friendly, just replace the object's color with its starting letter, as in, "I spy with my little eye something that starts with S." (Bonus tip: When your child spies something that's blue or starts with S, guess "sky." It's almost always the sky.) Whoever guesses correctly gets to go next!

3. **Packing List:** Our daughter introduced this fun memory-testing game to us after learning about it at school. One person starts by saying, "I'm going on a camping trip, and I'm bringing . . ." whatever thing the person feels like bringing, like "a tent." Then the second person repeats what the first person said and adds a second item to the packing list. Then the third person adds a third item, and so on. This continues as long as your group wants it to, leading to some hilariously long lists like "I'm going on a camping trip, and I'm bringing a tent, a canoe, hot dogs, a hairbrush, marshmallows, a telephone pole, a crazy monkey-man, a duffel bag full of crisp twenty-dollar bills, Dijon mustard, a bathtub, a humidifier, a dehumidifier, a bunch of bananas, a king-sized waterbed, and one clean pair of socks."

Listen to audiobooks

We're sure you've perfected an impressive playlist of kid-approved songs to listen to every time your family hits the road. But if you ever want a break from rockin' out to "I Am a Pizza," consider adding a children's audiobook or podcast to the mix. Kids love hearing stories even when they don't have pictures to look at, and doing so can help build their vocabulary, comprehension skills, and ability to visualize stories as they listen. Look for free children's podcasts online or explore your local library's audiobook collection.

Going to the store

Does it seem like parenting is mostly just trying to accomplish an endless list of errands while the crying, complaining kid accompanying you desperately attempts to stop you? If you want to raise a bookmonster, it's a good idea to change your perspective on that. Try viewing your child not as a nuisance who makes your chores take longer but as a conversation partner who makes them more fun. It'll be good for their language skills—and your sanity!

Write shopping lists together

Errands are easier when you plan ahead. Give your kid some extra writing practice by letting them help you jot down lists of the places you need to stop, and the things you need to buy. They'll enjoy being allowed to assist with such an important job, entertain you with precious misspellings like BROKLY and SEERUP, and maybe even help you get a little bit more organized.

Get them engaged

Stores are full of language development opportunities, so make sure you point them out to your bookmonster. In your casual conversations, you can give your kid practice with unusual vocabulary words ("What are kumquats anyway?"), letter and number recognition ("Let's see if we can find aisle 27"), reading ("We can't get that cereal because the first three ingredients are all sugar, see?"), writing ("You get to cross off the items on our list when we put them in the cart!"), and lots more. Plus, getting your child involved in accomplishing the errand itself might help stave off the boredom that would otherwise inevitably lead to throwing things out of your cart and running away from you in the store.

Eating out at restaurants

We get it. The thought of trying to keep your wee wild one calm and quiet for an entire meal in a nice restaurant might be giving you a panic attack right now. But remember that bookmonsters love channeling their energy into reading, and restaurants offer lots of ways to do just that.

Read the menu

You might be tempted to simply skim the menu yourself and then tell your kid what the choices are. But by holding the menu in front of them and pointing to the words as you say them, you'll show that there's real value in being able to read it all by yourself.

Read the check, too

Just in case you want your little animal to know how much freaking money it costs to feed them.

Ask for the crayons

Let's face it. You're probably not frequenting many five-star restaurants with the family. So when your waiter plops the paper placemats down on the table, use them to write pictures, letters, and words, or play fun games like Hangman while you wait for your food.

Talk

Remember that just having conversations with your kid is a great way to build vocabulary skills. So go ahead and talk it up! (Just try not to do it with your mouth full.)

Wherever there are signs

Written words out there in the world are powerful. They can tell us simple things like which door leads to the restroom or more complicated concepts like how to behave. We love it when we're with our kids and find the rules posted on signs, because it makes our parenting job easier.

We first learned this when we took our oldest kiddo (who was then just a toddler) to an ice cream shop with a little basketball game play area. The hoop was surrounded by a fence with a big sign on it that said DO NOT CLIMB OR CROSS OVER THIS FENCE. Of course, every single kid in the place wanted to climb in anyway, including ours. That is, until we pointed to the sign and read it out loud to her. Once she realized that staying behind the fence was a rule important enough to make a sign about, she stopped whining, and started working on her three-point shots instead. If you want your kid to follow the rules and avoid meltdowns, just try reading the signs!

Any place at all

Here's one thing you'll definitely want to get in the habit of: bringing books everywhere you go. They're portable, quiet, and never need to be recharged. They can keep kids occupied for hours. And they'll be building their bookmonster brains the whole time.

Make the decision today to make books your family's go-to entertainment option. Stock a box of books next to the car seat, let your kid choose a few to bring into restaurants, and stick some in your Mom or Dad bag to pull out in waiting rooms, during picnics at the park, or anywhere else the mood strikes. You can even make a separate excursion just for reading. Amber's absolute favorite outing with the kids is going to a coffee shop, letting each person pick out a "special drink" (non-caffeinated for the kiddos and maximum strength for Mommy), and sitting down to share a good book between sips.

10

Screen Time for Bookmonsters

In nature, animals must protect their young from all sorts of dangerous predators—bears, crocodiles, spiders, owls, sharks, piranhas, and tsetse flies, just to name a few. Parents of bookmonsters have to fend off threats to their book-loving little ones as well. And the most prevalent, persistent predator facing families of bookmonsters today is the kind that comes with a screen.

Screens are everywhere these days, from televisions, to movie theaters, to laptops, to tablets, to e-readers, to phones, to watches, to cars, to billboards, to airplanes, to taxi cabs, to gas pumps, to restaurants, to retail stores, to amusement parks, to refrigerators, to washing machines, to picture frames, to games, to toys, and probably to lots of other things that don't yet have screens on them at the time we're writing this, but will by the time you're reading it. Each of these screens is chock-full of digital information and visually exciting entertainment vying for our kids' attention. In fact, according to one study, children ages 0 to 8 spend nearly 500 percent more of their non-school hours staring at screens versus reading books.

So the average child looks at screens far more frequently than books. Is this a problem? If so, how big? And what the heck can anybody do about it anyway?

Assessing the threat

As anyone with a smartphone can tell you, managing screen time is difficult even for adults. It's all too easy to get so caught up in scrolling and swiping that we forget to interact with the world around us IRL (that means "in real life," for those of you who don't constantly use text-speak). But as annoying as the problem can be for us, it's absolutely critical for our children. Although our adult brains are already filled with knowledge and the ability to think critically, children's brains are still developing.

A young child's brain is far more active than an adult's as it is constantly at work making new neurological connections and setting itself up for more advanced forms of cognition. Daily experiences continuously affect this process, and the information that children take in—both on- and off-screen—will ultimately shape how they learn to think and behave. Because the experiences children have by age ten will have such a lasting, life-altering impact on their brains, making these experiences as positive as possible is kind of a no-brainer.

That's why it's important to understand that screen time is usually *not* the most brain-boosting way for children to spend their days. Here's why:

Screens can interfere with interaction

The more time your child spends watching screens, the less time they spend talking with you. This is a really big deal, since it's through your everyday conversations that children gain basic vocabulary and language skills that will help them become successful readers. Seriously—every time you open your mouth, gesture, nod, or simply listen to what your child has to say, the literacy-building benefits are basically impossible to beat.

Screens can decrease the ability to think deeply

Thanks to screen-based technology like internet-connected smartphones, people consume far more content than ever before—reading thousands of words per day from various news articles, emails, texts, social media posts, funny cat videos, and the like. But the way people read on a device differs dramatically from how we engage with print media. On a device, we tend to scroll quickly through text, scan for bolded headlines and bullet points, and let our eyes zigzag rapidly across the screen instead of concentrating on what we're reading line by line. As a result, we are less likely to think meaningfully about information, and we're less likely to remember what we've read. Since the same is true for children, too much time on devices can impede their ability to pay close attention to, reflect on, and think critically about the media they consume—all skills that are prerequisites for becoming good students and good citizens.

Screens can stifle basic brain skills

Exposure to too much non-educational television has been linked to poorer executive function—a term used to describe a variety of basic cognitive skills, including the ability to pay attention, tune out distractions, think flexibly, consider multiple perspectives on the same issue, keep lots of information in mind while solving problems, and resist impulsive behaviors. Executive function is basically everything a child needs to be able to sit still, listen, and learn—so it plays a huge role in school success beginning as early as kindergarten.

Screens can't teach as well as you might think

If you're convinced that none of these concerns apply to you because you only show your child "educational programming," we're about to become a real buzzkill. Study after study has compared children's ability to learn a concept from a prerecorded person on a television screen versus a live person in the same room. Even when the screen shows a video that re-creates exactly what the live person is doing, the live person still proves to be a more effective teacher. Every. Single. Time.

Does this mean that kids doing distance-learning classes via video conference are doomed to learn nothing? Not necessarily. The reason live teachers outperform prerecorded ones has a lot to do with the fact that they're able to interact with the kids on a one-on-one, personal level. As long as children are exposed to an attentive, responsive teacher on the other side of the screen (instead of a non-interactive puppet or cartoon character), their ability to learn should greatly improve.

Screens can totally eat up your time

Whether it's binge-watching TV shows, staying up all night to conquer video games, or frequenting your social media feeds, screen time can easily become a habit—or worse, an addiction. Even if your bookmonster's screen usage never reaches such obviously harmful extremes, it will still reduce the amount of time they could otherwise spend with books, siblings, or any number of more beneficial experiences.

Deterring attacks

Fortunately, we've got some ideas for how modern parents can defend kids from all these screens competing for their attention. Follow these tips, and you stand a halfway decent chance of preventing your budding bookmonster from becoming a zoned-out zombie:

Confine screens to common areas

It's easier to monitor what your child watches and how much time they spend on screens when they're located in shared spaces like dens and family rooms. But when televisions and computers are in children's bedrooms, it becomes much more difficult to ensure they're being used responsibly. Many studies have investigated the effect of in-bedroom screens on children's outcomes, and the results are overwhelmingly poor. Kids with screens in their rooms tend to spend more time using them, engage less in physical activity, have higher levels of obesity, and get less and lower quality sleep. So if you want your bookmonster to be a success, shut down the screen sleepovers ASAP!

Set time limits

The more time your bookmonster spends on screens, the less time they have for other stuff—like talking, reading, playing, and *not* shining lights directly into their eyeballs from three inches away. Screens can be such attractive time wasters that it's easy to let children whittle the hours away without hardly even noticing. And when kids are constantly stimulated by screens, they're more likely to become bored when the screens are off. Be purposeful about structuring screen time limits—per day, per week, or both—and then make sure your family sticks to them.

Also consider establishing completely device-free times or screen-free zones in your home. Researchers have (alarmingly) discovered that your interaction with another person can suffer by simply having your phone on the table in front of you—even if you aren't using it! It's one example of the all-too-common phenomenon of "technoference": Just the threat that something more interesting or important than the present company might pop up on your screen puts a damper on your conversation and interferes with your relationship. Show your loved ones you care by purposefully putting the screens away during regular routines—mealtimes, getting ready for bed, family game night, or whatever specific times work for you and your crew. If you can't think of any regular daily family routines, then it's the perfect time to create some—and be sure to make them screen-free from the start!

Turn off the TV when "no one is watching it"

If you're the type of person who leaves the television on after your show ends, you might want to think about powering it down more often. Researchers watching parents play with kids in both a quiet room and a room with a TV playing in the background found that families did significantly less talking when the TV was on. It seems that when a TV is making noise, people let it do the talking for them. And children's language and literacy skills suffer as a result.

Even more concerning is the finding that families who frequently have the television on as background noise get into the habit of talking to each other less in general. They talk less at home when the TV is on, but they also talk less when they leave the house and there isn't even a TV around! That adds up to a lot less language heard by the children in these families. So try turning off your TV when no one is watching, and make some noise of your own instead!

Depend less on devices

If the thought of trying to keep your kid quiet and well-behaved at a restaurant, in a store, or on an airplane terrifies you, you're not alone. Every parent worries about their little ones throwing gigantic temper tantrums from time to time. And to prevent potential meltdowns, plenty of moms and dads make a habit out of shoving screens in their kids' hands every time they go out in public.

Before you decide to join this trend of letting technology be your babysitter, consider this: Actions like engaging in mealtime conversation or sitting quietly with your own thoughts are skills that improve with practice. If your child never tries those things, they'll never get better at them, which will only end up hurting them in the long run. Plus, if you solely rely on electronic devices to keep your kid calm, what in the living heck are you going to do when the battery dies before your plane even reaches its cruising altitude of 35,000 feet? An initially tougher—yet ultimately smarter—strategy would be to challenge youngsters to behave more like the responsible big kids they're becoming. Encourage them to engage in polite conversation with their voices at an appropriate volume. Bring battery-free books for reading or papers for coloring if they want another way to stay entertained. And treat your tablet as an absolute last resort.

Model your own appropriate media use

One of the biggest predictors of children's screen time is how much time their parents spend on screens. Smartphones are an irresistible draw to even the tiniest tykes—in part because they have super fun buttons to push, but also because they see us parents holding them all the time. And what we're interested in, our kids are automatically interested in too.

That's why all our suggestions to emphasize books, stories, and talking with your kiddo, while simultaneously setting healthy limits for screen time, really apply to you as well. The more *you* model literacy-loving behaviors, the more *your kid* will get into those things as well. After all, the bookmonster doesn't fall far from the tree. (Or something like that!)

Picking your battles

Let's be real. Unless you're prepared to move to a farm, shut off your electricity, and have your fam go full-blown Amish, you won't be able to completely eliminate screens from your life. That's why it's important to be purposeful about screens, sharing them with your kiddo in deliberate ways that best promote educational skills and responsible use. Here are some ways to do just that.

Identify the kid-friendliest content

Up until now, we've mostly been warning you about the dangers of too much screen time. But there is encouraging evidence that kids can learn some pretty cool stuff by engaging with screens too, including enhanced visual and spatial skills, as well as educational content found in many children's shows, movies, and games. Just keep in mind that not all "educational programming" is created equal—so try to pick content that is:

- **Slow.** Have you noticed that some shows present information very quickly, with lots of movement and quick cuts between shots, while other shows display the information much . . . more . . . slowly? We know that slow-paced educational TV can seem interminable to adult viewers, but while we grown-ups are resisting the urge to yell "Get on with it already," our kids are using the time to better process the information they're viewing.

- **Repetitive.** Just as reading the same books more than once can reinforce concepts and help children learn more from the experience, consuming the same media repeatedly can help them understand it better as well.

- **Realistic.** Part of the challenge of learning from on-screen media is that kids have to make the connection between what they see on the screen and its connection to real objects and concepts from their actual lives. When the media is a more realistic visual match to their real lives, this leap is easier to make.

- **Age-Appropriate.** This should probably go without saying, but we're going to say it anyway. Whenever possible, steer kids away from cartoons, games, and shows that feature violent content, since they can lead to higher levels of aggression and a desensitization to real-life violence.

- **Interactive.** Kids get so much out of conversations with you because their actions truly affect what's happening in front of them. (Like, they scream at the top of their lungs, and you wince in pain.) Passive screen time options like watching TV offer none of those benefits. For example, *Dora the Explorer* is going to say "Gracias" for helping her at the end of every episode, even if your child didn't answer any of the questions she asked. But research shows that when a true interactive element is added to screen time, kids can benefit more. Consider choosing technologies like educational games that react to kids' clicks and taps, internet searches that allow kids to dream up a question and then find its answer, and video chats that facilitate interaction with people who are responsive to the things your kid says and does. (We're sure Grandma and Grandpa will be happy to help with that last one!)

Engage with e-books

These days many children's books come in electronic versions. These e-books are pretty handy in that you can buy and download them instantly, you can store a whole bunch of them on a single space-saving device, and they're potentially a positive, literacy-building way to appease a kid who's clamoring for more screen time. If you're thinking about giving e-books a try, here are some tips for making the most of your reading experience:

- **Read it like a regular book.** Book reading is so great for kids because of all the rich conversations you have while you're reading. The same things are important when you're reading e-books! Discuss all the things you normally would, like the thoughts and motivations of the characters, the setting of the story, connections between the book and your own real lives, and any of the other ideas from our "The Right Way to Read to a Bookmonster" chapter (see page 54).

- **Don't get too hung up on the tech.** Research shows that when technology is involved, parents often spend too much time talking about the mechanical logistics of the device itself, instead of remembering to have the more natural, skill-building dialogue that usually accompanies the shared reading of a physical book.

- **Support comprehension.** Although kids sometimes like how easy it is to scroll and skim through a digital book, those qualities make it harder to retain the information they read. Studies have shown that both kids and adults struggle to understand and remember electronic books compared to physical ones. So when talking about the digital books you read with your bookmonster, be sure to recall and reiterate important parts of the story.

- **Beware the "read to me" feature.** Although some electronic books will read aloud to your kid, it's no replacement for a real, live person. When you read aloud, you're aware of what your child is doing—when they're paying attention (or not), what they're understanding (or not), and which parts of the story they find most entertaining (or not). Because of this, you can do all the conversing, joke making, and gesturing that will really help your child get the most from the story. That's stuff an e-book could never do. And without it, there's no reason to assume your child is doing the kind of deep thinking about a text that can really teach literacy skills. While there's nothing wrong with an e-book reading to your child for entertainment, it's vital that you spend some serious time doing it too.

- **Remember that screens can't replace physical books.** E-books are fun, interactive, and can really save on shelf space, but remember to keep plenty of the old-fashioned ones on hand too. A physical book has an important presence in your home, because it's always there for your child to easily see, touch, open, experience—and return to again and again and again.

Learning to coexist

As your child grows up and starts using screens more, the single biggest thing you can do to help them make the most of screen time and maintain a healthy love of learning is this: Consume digital media *together*. When you interact with your kid about the television they're viewing and the video games they're playing, they'll be able to learn much more from the experience.

You may be surprised at how little children learn from using media on their own, even when the content is educational. To adults, educational games and shows seem obviously beneficial—just look at all those letters, words, and numbers, after all! But to young kids who don't already know everything there is to know about each of those educational concepts, absorbing fast, fully animated lessons flying rapid-fire out of a screen might feel a whole lot harder.

Try sitting with your child while they watch or play with screens. Doing so gives you the opportunity to reinforce or explain education-al concepts they might otherwise be missing, while also adding the all-important element of interaction that screen time rarely provides. An easy way to start is by simply reading words aloud when they ap-pear on screen. Even shows and movies geared toward young children often include on-screen text that non-readers would completely miss out on, and cuing kids into it can enhance their understanding and enjoyment of the story. Every time we've watched a movie with one of our kids who wasn't reading independently yet, we'd be sure to vocal-ize and explain things like signs, newspaper headlines, and even the opening credits—"Universal Pictures. That's the company that made the movie. *Despicable Me 3*. That's the movie we're seeing! Oh, and these are all names of the people whose voices are in the movie. Cool, huh?" Doing this kind of thing has the added effect of constantly rein-forcing the idea that print is interesting and informative—wherever it is found.

Another benefit of sharing screen time is that it will help you stay connected to your child's ever-changing interests. You can bond over conversations about what they're watching, why they like it, how they would improve it if they could, and more. You can also relate the con-tent to your real-life experiences and the books you've read together. That way, screen time can benefit book time and vice versa—rath-er than the two competing for your kid's attention. Remember that anything can be a springboard for a good conversation, including a video game, movie, or show.

We understand that you can't always be right there next to your bookmonster, guiding them through their on-screen adventures. So be strategic about how you use screens. If you don't plan on making screen time interactive, schedule it for a time when you wouldn't be interacting with your child anyway. Like if you know you need to clean up, make phone calls, do work, or engage in some all-too-rare parent-only time behind your locked and barricaded bedroom door, go ahead and throw on a show or two. If you keep that time relatively short (insert Dad performance joke here) and spend lots of other time during the day interacting together, then screens don't have to stop your bookmonster from growing gargantuan reading skills.

Books + screens = serious family fun!

Want to know our family's very favorite way to make screen time benefit reading time? Read a book together . . . and then watch the movie version. Our kids love it, and so do we!

Many children's books that are turned into movies are long chapter books, so if your kid is still little, you might not think they're ready for this kind of thing. But we found that our kids have enjoyed reading chapter books with us even as young as two years old. Just go into it knowing that it will take days or weeks to read the whole thing, and remember that you can always pause the story to explain bigger words or more complex ideas whenever you need to.

Here are some reasons that reading the book *before* seeing the movie is the way to go:

It subdues the scary parts

We secretly relish it when our kids get extra cuddly with us during a movie's scarier moments. But it's also nice that they're never *too* freaked out when watching a movie version of a book we've read, since they know the characters are going to end up OK. It also helps to remind them of that fact over and over before the show starts.

Kids look forward to their favorite parts

After weeks of reading together, kids will delight in the opportunity to see their favorite jokes, characters, and scenes played out on-screen.

You get to talk about what you thought

Seeing the movie version makes for lots of fun conversation about how the movie was the same as, or different from, what we'd read and imagined.

There are many great book-movie combos out there for your family to share. Here are some of the ones our family has broken out the popcorn for:

- *Charlie and the Chocolate Factory* by **Roald Dahl**
  This book has *two* movie versions to try, so your family members can decide if they're on Team Wilder or Team Depp. (For the record, our family is definitely *not* all on the same team!)

- *Cloudy with a Chance of Meatballs* by **Judi Barrett**
  The book leans heavily on illustrations and is really light on plot, so it's cool to see how much the truly funny movie adds to fill out a full ninety minutes.

- *Holes* by Louis Sachar

  With a plot that crosses continents and generations and still somehow manages to make every single detail a vital component of the story, this book is truly a work of art. It includes some difficult concepts like racism, violence, and death, but reading it together offers you the chance to guide your kiddo through those parts and explain your own values about them.

- The Harry Potter series by J. K. Rowling

  Featuring kids who have the power to fly on broomsticks, create magic potions, and stay up way past their bedtimes, these are sure to be a hit with all witch and wizard wannabes! But beware: the books, and especially the movies, get darker and scarier the further along you go—so think about what your child can handle, and be generous with your snuggles!

- *The BFG* by Roald Dahl

  There are so many entertaining Roald Dahl book-to-movie adaptations that we had to include a second one on the list! Joke-loving bookmonsters will appreciate hearing all the Big Friendly Giant's silly, mixed-up word mispronunciations in ear-blasting surround sound.

- The Captain Underpants series by Dav Pilkey

  This series of books twice topped the American Library Association's list of most banned books, so it's clearly not for everyone. But the plentiful potty jokes, silly scenarios, and crazy characters running around in their underwear make lots and lots of kids super excited to read—and those are some underpants we can definitely get behind!

11

Playtime for Bookmonsters

Bats aren't actually blind. Camels don't really store water in their humps. And no matter how many billowing matadors' capes suggest otherwise, bulls couldn't care less about the color red. People believe misconceptions about all sorts of animals out there—including an awfully big one about bookmonsters.

Close your eyes for a moment and think about what "a child who reads lots of books" looks like. What did you imagine? If you pictured a lonely, quiet kid, head buried in a book beneath a solitary bedroom reading lamp for hours on end, we wouldn't blame you. It's a common image many of us have seen in movies and TV shows since our own childhoods. But here's the thing: That is most certainly *not* the species that this book is all about! Unlike the passive, introverted "bookworm" stereotypes many of us parents grew up with, today's bookmonsters are active, engaged, fun-loving creatures who use reading to inspire play, and play to inspire reading.

That's right! You no longer need to choose between raising a child who likes to read or who likes to have fun. Who is thoughtful or playful. Who gets good grades or gets good at sports. Because bookmonsters can do all those things—all at once! Remember that bringing up bookmonsters is not about formal, sit-down reading lessons. It's about making reading an activity your kid will love throughout their life. And one of the most effective ways to do that is to associate reading with playing!

In a time when families are more overscheduled than ever, it's important to remember to prioritize time for play. Here are just a few of the many, many reasons why:

Play is healthy

Active play promotes physical health, exploratory play promotes cognitive development, and interactive play with friends and family is great for the psyche.

Play is empowering

Play gives children the opportunity to determine their own course of action and freely express themselves. For young kids who have very little control over the rest of their schedule, it's a unique time to be the boss.

Play is work

Kids learn from exploring and interacting with their environment—something they're naturally motivated to do from birth. Play is a time for kids to test hypotheses and try out new ideas when the stakes are as minimal (and exciting) as knocking over a tower of blocks.

Play is effective

Kids acquire long-lasting lessons from play they just can't learn in any other way. Research studies comparing preschool programs find no lasting advantage for kids in highly academic versus play-based schools. In fact, kids in more rigorous programs sometimes fare worse in areas like creativity, emotional well-being, and social development.

Play is fun!

And really, is there any better reason?

Since all kids love to play, the surest way to bring up a bookmonster is to add literacy-building behaviors to playtime. Some of the strategies for doing this are obviously connected to reading, while others aren't. Keep your mind open to the idea that even play activities that seem to have little to do with literacy can in fact provide a big boost to book skills. And if you do this right, your kid will have so much fun, they won't even realize how much they're learning.

Get your games on

Playing games as a family is custom-made for promoting a bookmonster's skills. Many board and card games are intentionally focused on letters and reading, and even those that aren't tend to get everyone engaged in lots of vocabulary-building conversations. Who knows—an overly competitive grandparent might even expose everyone to colorful, old-timey swear words like "dadgummit."

Research shows that children from families who engage in frequent, conversation-rich activities like playing games together enjoy benefits like larger vocabularies, higher reading scores, more motivation in school, and a more positive perception of the parent-child relationship. One day your kid's memories of childhood will be made up of the experiences that were your regular family traditions, so if you aren't doing it already, go ahead and institute a family game night . . . or game day . . . or just squeeze in a quick game whenever you have some downtime!

Here are just a few of our family's favorites:

Tic-Tac-Toe

Admittedly, the literary value of this game is minimal, but at least it helps kids distinguish between Xs and Os. It's also easy to play a quick game anytime you have a pencil and paper, or a crayon and a restaurant placemat, or a sandy beach and your big toe. (Wonder if that's where it got its name?)

Telephone

This game—where players try to whisper the same message from one person to another but inevitably get it all wrong—is more fun the worse your group is at it. And while you talk and laugh about how crazy the whispered message became, you're really teaching your kid lessons about how words with very different meanings can be pronounced and spelled in very similar ways.

Hangman

Guessing letters to fill in the blanks of a mystery word or phrase is perfect for kids who have started reading already. But after seeing how much her big brother and sister were loving this game, even our three-year-old wanted to play. She proudly drew blanks all over her whiteboard, then filled in letters and squiggles at random until we'd guessed everything in the alphabet. A D _ R A B _ E !

Charades

Even though the person performing in this classic party game never speaks, it always leads to loads of loud fun. Plus, there are tons of language lessons to learn, from touching your arm to break down words into individual syllables, to tugging your ear to indicate a rhyming word that "sounds like" the clue, to giving everybody practice with symbolic gestures that stand for words like *book*, *song*, and *movie*.

Apples to Apples

This card-collecting game is perfect for expanding kids' vocabularies, as every card contains a key word that all players are trying to win, along with multiple synonyms for it.

Bears vs. Babies

Full warning: If you don't feel comfortable encouraging your kid to build powerful monsters designed to eat invading armies of horrible babies, then this game isn't for you. But if you're cool with it (like we are), then get ready to giggle incessantly as you and your kid take turns combining cards to make creatures like "A Pomeranian of Light and Wonder Wearing Incredible Underpants" and "A Velociraptor Who Is Also a Tank." The more hilarious things you read, the more everybody will crack up!

Instructions

No, we're not referring to some obscure game called "Instructions" that you've never heard of. We're talking about the *actual instructions* for whatever game you happen to be playing. As anybody who has ever played games with us knows, Andy has a special affinity for reading all the rules, and then explaining them to all players in painstaking detail.

We're not saying you have to go to his yawn-inducing extreme, but we are saying that it's a good idea to show your kid the instructions sheet and talk a bit about why it's important. When bookmonsters see you read the rules and point out exciting specifics like, "It says here that the youngest player gets to go first," they learn firsthand that written words have the power to create wonderful, fun experiences.

Take it outside

All kids need regular playtime outside to run around and exercise their bodies. But just because outside play is physical doesn't mean it can't be mental, too! Here are some ideas for incorporating language education into your outdoor activities:

Ride bikes

Our family loves to bike to local restaurants, parks, the beach, the movies, and anywhere else that isn't so far we need a car. These beloved outings aren't a break from being bookmonsters but rather a fun opportunity to bring language and literacy along with us. There are always plenty of one-way, street name, and stop signs to point out and read when we're on the road. Plus, when we park, our kids' bike locks force them to get a little reading in. Instead of a traditional number combination lock, we opted for ones that use letters—which allowed our kids to choose any four-letter word they wanted to be the "key" to unlock their bikes. We won't reveal their secret combos here, but trust us that the words they chose are weird and random and ones we would never have predicted. We bet you'll get a kick out of seeing which word your child is drawn to as well. The locks are great because they give our kids exposure to letters every time they lock and unlock their bikes, plus offer them the amusing activity of spinning the letters around and around to make more and more words. Like "poop." They recently discovered—and lamented—that they could've, would've, should've picked "poop."

Go for hikes

Fresh air, sunshine, and all sorts of fascinating plants and animals await your kid each time you go for a hike through nature. In addition to reading trailhead signposts and information markers you find along the way, you can also introduce your kiddo to new vocabulary words as you describe the area's geology, flora, and fauna. Or play a *sign-free* version of the Alphabet Game from the "Bookmonsters on the Loose" chapter (page 85) by pointing out objects whose names start with letters A to Z. If you're feeling brave enough, you can even hand your little one a map and let them lead the way!

Shoot some hoops

Basketball has been one of our family's favorite sports ever since our biggest bookmonster joined her third-grade team. One of the easiest basketball games you can play is also the bookmonster-iest: PIG. Players take turns shooting the ball, and when someone makes a basket, the next person has to shoot from the exact same place. Make it, and the game continues. Miss it, and you get your first letter, P. Miss a second and third shot that your opponent made, and you'll end up with P-I-G, and you're out of the game. People play PIG and the two-shots-longer game HORSE all the time, but when spelling words is this much fun, why stop there? Go crazy by choosing different animal (or non-animal) things to spell—like FOX,

PLATYPUS, or ROW, ROW, ROW YOUR BOAT. You'll be working out your muscles, and memories, with every shot!

Jump rope

Skipping rope by itself might not help you learn to read, but if you sing some classic jump rope rhymes while you hop, it definitely can! Memorable sing-alongs can tune your kid into the sounds of language, like the repetitive rhymes in *Miss Mary Mack Mack Mack, all dressed in black black black, with silver buttons buttons buttons, up and down her back back back.* Some songs even address the ABCs and spelling directly, like *Ice cream soda, cherry on top! Who's your best friend? I forgot. A, B, C, D, E, F, G . . .*—everyone keeps singing through the alphabet, and when the person in the middle misses a jump, they have to think of a friend's name that starts with that letter!

Chalk up the sidewalk

Sidewalk chalk is kind of like crayons' cool, streetwise, older cousin. It lets little ones expand their horizons past a little piece of paper on the kitchen table, and take their coloring game out into the big, wide world. And there's a world's worth of ways you can use it to improve your child's reading abilities. Write words that label the pictures you each draw, challenge your child to identify the letters and numbers you write, create your own hopscotch courts (using numbers *or* letters to hop to), write different words on the sidewalk and have your kid jump to the ones you call out, see how small you can write the word *small* and how big you can write the word *big*, and on and on until you run out of ideas (or it starts raining).

Turn fiction into reality

When you're reading books with your kid, let the characters' fun out-door activities inspire your real-life adventures. For example, *Cam Jansen and the Tennis Trophy Mystery* by David A. Adler might moti-vate you to grab a racket and get to your nearest tennis court, and J. K. Rowling's Harry Potter series might encourage you to take up the game of Quidditch. Now . . . where did you leave your magical flying broomstick?

Garden

Digging, planting, watering, weeding, picking, and eating stuff you grow in your own garden is a cool way to help your bookmonster get in touch with nature. And with lots of informative words on equip-ment like seed packets, fertilizers, and plant labels, it can help their reading skills grow, too!

Prep the equipment

Does your football, soccer ball, basketball, or bike tire need air before the games begin? Have your kid help you with the air pump! There's tons of unusual vocabulary to point out, read, and talk about while you're working. "It says to inflate to 8 PSI. Inflate means to fill with air. PSI means pounds per square inch, and if we do eight of those, we'll make sure the ball bounces really high without exploding." The best part, though, is when you tell them what it means to "moisten" a needle, and then totally gross them out by doing it with your own spit!

Play pretend

Some parents get weirded out when their children have imaginary friends, talk to stuffed animals like they have real thoughts and personalities, or seem to be constantly pretending about some crazy thing or other. But don't fret! This likely just shows that your child has good imaginative and social skills, which can mean very good things for their future reading abilities. Many research studies support the idea that pretend play promotes higher-level thinking skills that are required for reading, like:

Keeping multiple things in mind

When children create pretend scenarios, they have to juggle lots of ideas in their heads at once—like the parts they're playing, the plot they're enacting, and the props they're using. Doing this exercises kids' working memory skills, which they'll need to remember things they've read, comprehend test questions, and more.

Using symbols

When your child pretends a baby blanket is a row boat, they're using the blanket as a symbol for "boat." Language and reading use symbols, too, requiring children to learn that words are symbols for real things in the world, and letters are symbols for the language sounds they know.

Creating a story

Some pretend scenarios are short and simple (like sitting down for a basic tea party), while others are long and meandering (like when your tea party is crashed by a hungry dragon with a craving for pizza who strongly suggests that you convert your entire living room into a dragon-friendly, wood-fired pizzeria). The more practice with pretend play and exposure to imaginative books and stories that your child gets, the more elaborate, coherent, and totally cool their stories can become!

Want your kid to get even more out of pretend play? Try joining in yourself while looking for ways to subtly introduce learning opportunities into the pretend scenarios they've already started. For example, if your child is playing "restaurant," you can apply for a job, then encourage your new workplace to include aspects like creating menus, writing down orders, and adding up totals on customers' bills. Or next time your kiddo is playing "hair salon," you might show up as the mail carrier who delivers a stack of real magazines for them to put out and peruse in their waiting area.

Although it's a great idea to play with your kid like this often, you don't want to do it *all the time*. First, because dinner is not going to make itself. And second, because leaving children alone for independent playtime lets them discover and experiment for themselves in ways they can't when you're constantly hanging around. So fill your kid's play spaces with bookmonster-friendly materials like construction paper, notepads, easels, pens, pencils, markers, crayons, chalk, erasers, books, and toys that have printed text on them—and then get out of their way!

Picking the Proper Toys

Choosing letter-filled, literacy-building toys is another way to help your bookmonster get the most out of playtime. If your little one loves building with blocks, look for ones with letters on them. If they love dressing up as different characters, find costumes that could help transform them into their favorite storybook characters. If they're all about puzzles, there are tons of letter-themed ones to try. All our kids played with these cool wooden puzzles with pieces shaped like each letter of the alphabet, and a picture of a word that starts with that letter underneath each one—like a zebra hiding under the letter Z. Each time your kiddo picks up a new piece, you can say the name of the letter, the sound it makes, the name of the thing pictured, and as many other words that start with the letter as you want. We've also enjoyed letter magnets and letters that stick to the wall of the kids' bathtub. The best thing about these toys is that there are so many things kids can do with them: pair matching uppercase and lowercase letters together, spell words, sort letters by color, pretend the uppercase letters are the lowercase letters' Mommies and Daddies, and more.

For maximum enjoyment and education, you can't go wrong with open-ended toys. Unlike toys that are designed to have a single, best use—like a car for driving or a teapot for pouring tea—open-ended toys like balls, blocks, and clay are not for anything in particular and don't do much of anything on their own. But when kids use their imaginations with them, the uses are endless!

12

Bookmonsters Travel in Packs

Honeybees divide tasks like cleaning, reproducing, and finding food to get all their colony's jobs done. Geese fly in a V formation to save energy. And zebras stick together in large herds to confuse lions trying to pick out a single striped body to pounce on.

Bookmonsters benefit from hanging out in groups, too. Because kids are naturally social creatures, the relationships they form with friends are super important—and influential—to their development. This creates a huge opportunity for you: if you can get your kid and their friends to enjoy book-related fun together, then reading can become cool. Playdates and literacy skill building can be one and the same. And positive peer pressure can kick in, with the whole gang pushing and encouraging each other to develop a deeper and longer-lasting love of reading.

Books make friendships better

Here's a fun fact you may not have thought about before: Reading more can make your kid better at friendship! You see, every time bookmonsters read about the thoughts, feelings, struggles, and triumphs of a new character in a book, they learn what it's like to be a different person. Each new adventure they page-flip through is a chance to see the world from a new perspective and empathize with someone in a situation that may be very different from their own. This experience allows them to interact in ways that other people find welcoming, supportive, and entertaining—exactly the skills your kid needs to attract and maintain friendships!

For most children, the knowledge that other people have thoughts, feelings, and beliefs that are different from their own doesn't fully emerge until they're about five years old. But since it's been well-documented that kids who read more develop empathy earlier, parents can kick-start this process by reading books aloud often. The connection between more reading and better social skills continues throughout life, too, with research showing that adults who read more fiction score higher in measures of empathy compared to their non-reading peers. So be sure to keep reading even as an adult, since it could make you a better friend!

Ways to share words with friends

When our youngest daughter was three, we happened to overhear a charming exchange between her and a friend she had over for a playdate. The two girls were going to the bathroom together: our daughter using the little potty chair and her friend using the big toilet. To pass the time while they tinkled, they chatted, and since the door was ajar we got to hear some of it:

Our Daughter's Friend: "What's it says?"
Our Daughter: "I don't know. I think it says toilet paper."
Our Daughter's Friend: "Ohhhhh!"

Both kids clapped and cheered, and then emerged from the bathroom beaming—clearly satisfied with themselves for apparently cracking the code. We could tell that the girls had been talking about print, but we were also pretty sure nothing in the bathroom actually read "toilet paper." So we walked in, surveyed the scene, and realized the girls had been looking at the toilet paper roll, which was imprinted with a very tasteful flower pattern interspersed with the printed word "Charmin." The girls understood the toilet paper had words on it that said something, but since neither of them could read, they made their best guess as to what it must say.

Aside from making us sigh wistfully because we knew these precious little kiddos wouldn't stay this precious and little for long, this story also reminded us of a couple of things. First, it demonstrated that once children realize print conveys interesting meaning, they will be drawn to it and want to know what it says wherever they find it. (Even on toilet paper rolls.) And second, it showed that kids love to share print and reading with other people. They understand instinctively that if reading is fun by yourself and with parents, it's bound to be fun with friends, too!

Here are several easy ways you can incorporate literacy activities into your kid's playdates with peers—no toilet paper rolls required!

Add storytime to playdates

Kids can't resist books. Any kids. We know this because it never fails that when we're out in public reading books to our kids, any other children in the general vicinity will begin slowly sidling over until we're all huddled together enjoying the story. So you shouldn't resist books, either. Help make books a regular part of playtime with friends by pausing free-play sessions for storytime just like you would break for snack time. It will be an especially genius move if you happen to time it at one of those inevitable moments when you sense the kids are getting bored or getting into a fight.

Celebrate birthdays with a good book

Planning a party? Consider adding storytime to your list of activities. Hired entertainers like princesses and mermaids often include this as part of their act, but you can easily do the reading yourself if you don't feel like breaking the bank. Think about choosing a book that matches your party theme, and maybe even send kids home with a copy of the book as their party favor. Unlike the typical goodie bags full of nonsense that end most children's parties, parents won't have to fish your books out of the cracks of the couch and throw them away a few days later.

Give the gift of books

Invited to some *other* kid's birthday party? You know there will be tons and tons of toys to unwrap—so think about giving the gift of a special book or two instead. Get your bookmonster involved by asking which books they think their friend would really like. And remember that books make great gifts during the holidays, too!

Start a book club

Often after the thrilling, emotional experience of reading a good book, you're bursting to talk about it. But unless you happen to know someone else who's also read it, you're usually out of luck. That's why book clubs are so great—they turn a typically individual activity into a special social occasion. So why not introduce your kid to the joy of discussing books with friends by helping them form a book club of their own? It's easy—all you need are at least two willing participants, a book you've agreed to read, a place to meet up after you've read it, and of course some snacks. (Bonus if the snacks are inspired by the book!)

Think your kid is too young for book clubs? Don't be so sure. Our children's elementary school runs a school-wide book club of sorts, where teachers in all the classrooms from kindergarten through fifth grade read the same book aloud to their students during the same month. The books always feature a positive behavior theme like respect or honesty, and concepts from the book are reinforced through book-centered activities at regularly scheduled school-wide assemblies. Kids in every classroom enjoy hearing and talking about the stories, plus the books provide a common vocabulary for addressing playground issues.

Swap stories

We love getting new books and have amassed a pretty giant library of them at home—but nobody can buy all the books they want. That's why we frequently offer to trade books with friends. Just bag up some of your well-read favorites and trade them for a bag of books your friends have selected from their home library. Borrowing new stories your kid hasn't read before will be exciting, and getting yours back after they've been gone awhile will make the familiar old stories feel fresh again.

Use books to inspire play

Some books are so suited to reenacting with friends that they almost seem like recipes for playdates. In *Fancy Nancy: Ooh La La! It's Beauty*

Day by Jane O'Connor, Nancy and her sister set up a fancy spa in their backyard and treat their mom to a day full of pampering. The book even includes a detailed description of fancy accessories you can use to decorate your spa, instructions about how to re-create your own spa treatments, and tips for snacks to serve—making it ultra-easy for your little Fancy Nancy fan to replicate the experience with friends!

Family Members Are Friends, Too

Although we've mainly been talking about your kid's friends in this chapter, let's not forget about the first friends they ever made—family! All the book-reading, story-sharing, and game-playing experiences we've mentioned are perfect for your child to share with siblings and cousins, too.

Siblings in particular can benefit greatly from sharing books and language with one another. Younger kids can take in healthy doses of book-loving peer pressure while watching their older siblings read. Older kids can delight in sharing their favorite board books and simple stories with their growing little sibs. And the whole family can enjoy the fact that frequent positive interactions with books leave the kids with less time for fighting, and more time for building happy, healthy bonds that last a lifetime!

PART III

Feeding Your Growing Bookmonster

Just like your kid needs nutritious foods to grow healthy skin, bones, and muscles, your bookmonster needs a steady diet of language and literacy morsels to develop a ferocious, lifelong appetite for books and learning. This next group of chapters is all about equipping you with a "grocery list" full of materials, activities, and talking points you'll want to stock up on to make sure you're supplying all the nourishment your bookmonster needs. The books, jokes, games, puns, and memory activities you're about to read are sure to get any bookmonster salivating!

13

The Best Books for Your Bookmonster

Giant panda meals are 99 percent bamboo. Monarch caterpillars consume nothing but milkweed. And black-footed ferrets eat over one hundred prairie dogs each year. Such simple and repetitive diets seem to be working out fine for all those animals (except the prairie dogs, of course). But bookmonsters do best when they eat lots of very different things.

You see, when it comes to wolfing down the written word, bookmonsters are true omnivores. They can't just read a single type of book over and over again—they need to sample generously from the entire book buffet. By consuming as many different kinds of writing as they can, kids develop a healthy, well-balanced diet that will expose them to a variety of ideas, help them discover which writing styles they find most engaging, and set them up to get the most out of their lifelong love affair with reading.

So as you go through the constantly evolving process of selecting reading material for your little one, remember that variety is truly the spice of a young bookmonster's life. Go ahead and get books you know will be popular because they're similar to ones your kid has liked before, but don't be afraid to try new things. If you push yourself to explore titles outside your family's typical comfort zone, you might find an author, book series, or genre that captures your child's imagination and sends their excitement about reading to a whole new level.

Balancing your bookmonster's diet

Now that you know the importance of diversity in your bookmonster's diet, it's time to start shopping for ingredients. There are many more categories of books out there than you may realize. To help you hunt and gather everything you need to nourish your little one's growing appetite, check out our handy "Book Pyramid" here.

Ask yourself: Which categories do you and your child read from a lot? Which ones may be a little neglected? Are there any that you've never even tried? A bookmonster's ideal home library contains multiple servings from each of these groups—so that whenever your kid is hungry for a good book, finding something to satisfy that craving will be easy. Keep reading for detailed descriptions of each category, including specific book titles that fall into each one. For maximum health and happiness, make sure to sample a little something from every part of the Book Pyramid!

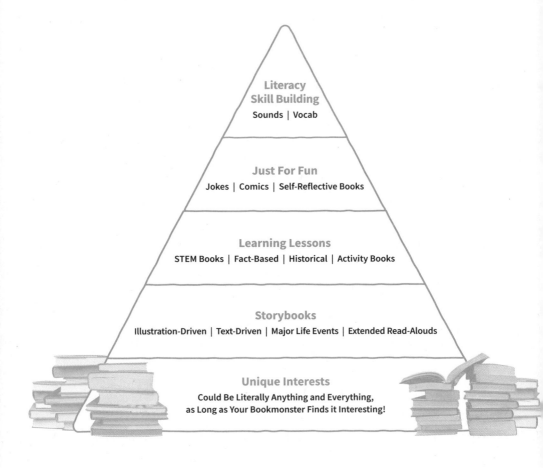

Literacy skill building

The first books that every aspiring reader needs are ones that build literacy skills, including becoming familiar with letters, understanding the sounds of language, and learning the meanings of words. While any book your child picks up will do this to some degree, some books target particular literacy skills especially well.

Playing with sounds

Kids' books are full of alliteration, rhymes, and other examples of the sounds that words and letters make. (So read some of these, for goodness' sake!)

A Nibble

Green Eggs and Ham by Dr. Seuss
Of all Dr. Seuss's rhymes, our family has enjoyed this one the most. Maybe it's because we have our own Sam in the family, or because we love eggs, or because we're all real hams ourselves, or because its rhyme repetitions are extra catchy. Whatever the reason, we've been enjoying this book for years—beginning when our bookmonsters were just babies.

A Gobble

Where the Sidewalk Ends by Shel Silverstein
Here's a little-known fact about Andy: he once spent an entire year writing one poem about onion bagels every single day—that's 365 poems about a single breakfast food, people! So yeah, our family enjoys poetry. And Shel Silverstein's beloved books are so silly, whimsical, and hilarious that they're sure to get your family appreciating poetry, too.

More to Taste

Beastly Feasts! by Robert L. Forbes
I'm Just No Good at Rhyming: And Other Nonsense for Mischievous Kids and Immature Grown-Ups by Chris Harris
Jeepers Creepers: A Monstrous ABC by Laura Leuck
The Pout-Pout Fish by Deborah Diesen

Vocabulary building

When your child is little, basically every book contains new vocabulary words to learn. As they and their reading skills grow, look for books that push them to continuously add new words and phrases to their repertoires!

A Nibble

The Fancy Nancy series by Jane O'Connor
When our daughter got the first pink, frilly, sparkle-covered book in this series, we were afraid it would be nothing more than an overly cutesy story brimming with gender stereotypes. Oh boy, were we wrong! Yes, Nancy does love all things fancy, including traditionally girly clothing and accessories. But what she loves even more is fancy words! Nancy never shies away from using big words, and she overtly defines them by explaining that they're a "fancy" way to say other words your child already knows. (Like plume is a fancy word for feather!)

A Gobble

The Timmy Failure series by Stephan Pastis
For an elementary school student, Timmy Failure certainly has an impressive vocabulary. But when you run your very own detective agency, stuff like that comes in handy. Your kid will enjoy reading about Timmy's hilarious misadventures as he rides around town on his Segway with his polar bear best friend and a ragtag collection of human friends in tow. Since some of the vocabulary is advanced, we found that reading the books aloud together until our kids could understand them independently was a sure recipe for success.

More to Taste

Dinosaur Roar! by Paul and Henrietta Stickland
First 100 Words by Roger Priddy
Skippyjon Jones by Judy Schachner
The Word Collector by Peter H. Reynolds

Just for fun

The next type of book you'll want to share with your little one is the kind that makes them laugh! Lighthearted selections that don't take themselves too seriously—like joke books, comic books, and others—communicate to kids that reading can be undeniably fun. And since bookmonsters love reading so much partly because they see it as a super entertaining way to spend some time, you'll want them to get that message as soon as possible.

Worried that these kinds of books aren't sophisticated enough for your future academic all-star? You'll be happy to know that having fun with books *isn't* all fun and games. Studies show that when families read humorous books together, they tend to engage in higher-quality conversations about more complex ideas while using more advanced vocabulary. Because kids' language, reading, and academic skills benefit greatly from that type of interaction, funny books are fun *and* educational—and we can *seriously* support that!

Joke books

It's unbelievable how much fun a whole bunch of silly jokes can be when you're sharing them as a family!

A Nibble	*Laugh-Out-Loud Animal Jokes for Kids* by Rob Elliott We happened upon our family's first joke book in the gift section of our local pharmacy while we were waiting for a prescription to be filled. We figured we would waste a few minutes reading its corny knock-knock jokes and punny one-liners and then put it back on the shelf, but instead we found ourselves immediately hooked and had to bring it home.
A Gobble	*Riddles & Brain Teasers: Best Riddles for Challenging Smart Kids* by Rusty Cove-Smith Riddles combine the playfulness of jokes with the logic of puzzles, and are one of our kids' favorite ways to pass the time while waiting in restaurants, driving in the car, or any other time we're sitting around without much to do.
More to Taste	*Martha Speaks: Funny Bone Jokes and Riddles* by Karen Barss and Susan Meddaugh **The Just Joking books** by National Geographic Kids *The Super, Epic, Mega Joke Book for Kids* by Whee Winn

Comic books

Did your childhood include exciting mornings flipping through an actual newspaper to find the "funny pages," or trading superhero comic books at a real, live comic book store? Even though physical papers and rinky-dink retail shops like that are basically relics of the past nowadays, you can still share this nostalgic experience with your kid with book-length collections of current comics and your favorite classics.

A Nibble	***Hello Kitty: Delicious!*** by Jorge Monlongo Hello Kitty comic books like this one have almost no words, so you can either have a lively conversation about them, or let your kid enjoy them independently. The vivid pictures are a great introduction to comics, and they usually have sweet, easily accessible storylines.
A Gobble	***Garfield at Large*** by Jim Davis (and pretty much every other Garfield book that came after it) Our son became so hooked on this old-school, lasagna-loving cat that he had a Garfield-themed birthday party and gave Garfield books as favors to all his friends!
More to Taste	***Adventures in Cartooning*** by James Sturm, Andrew Arnold, and Alexis Frederick-Frost ***Narwhal: Unicorn of the Sea*** by Ben Clanton ***The Adventures of Super Diaper Baby*** by Dav Pilkey ***The Days Are Just Packed: A Calvin and Hobbes Collection*** by Bill Watterson

Self-reflective books

Concerned you'll get bored reading kids' books all the time? Books that understand and acknowledge the fact that they are books are the perfect way to shake you out of your routine. Plus, they're usually really funny!

A Nibble

Press Here by Hervé Tullet
As much activity as it is book, this read will entertain everyone! Each page offers kids a new way to interact with the book. They get to press the dot, tilt the book on its side, and shake it up. The best part is that the dot seems to respond to their actions!

A Gobble

More Bears! by Kenn Nesbitt
This personal family favorite is a story about a book being written . . . a book with absolutely no bears. That is, until the book's "readers" start demanding that the story have "More bears!" Your kid will dig yelling right along with the book and seeing it pay off as more and more bears are added to the story (until things get out of hand)!

More to Taste

Snappsy the Alligator (Did Not Ask to Be in This Book) by Julie Falatko
This Book Just Ate My Dog! by Richard Byrne
We Are in a Book! by Mo Willems

Learning lessons

Another group of books that will prove invaluable to your child throughout life is those that explain something educational. These books can contain nothing but facts (like almanacs and encyclopedias), tell fictional stories that happen to include elements of historical or scientific significance, or be simple page-turners that introduce young readers to basic concepts like numbers or shapes. These books are smart to have around your house now, since children who get early experience using factual books often find them easier to use and learn from when they need to rely on them as educational resources later. In a broader sense, these books will help your kid realize that if there's ever something that they don't understand, are curious about, or wish they knew better, reading a book is the answer!

STEM (Science, Technology, Engineering, and Math)

Since research shows that introducing children to STEM concepts early can help them achieve more success in those areas later, keep an eye out for fun-looking science and math titles to add to your home library.

A Nibble	**Grandma's Tiny House** by JaNay Brown-Wood Friends and family come to Grandma's house for a feast, and kids can count groups of uncles, cousins, neighbors, and others who bring equally countable items to contribute. This simple, adorable book will inspire interactions about numbers, celebrations, and the joys of family.
A Gobble	**The Zoey and Sassafras series** by Asia Citro Zoey discovers that she has the ability to see magical creatures and the responsibility to care for them when they need help. But since magical creatures don't come with manuals, she has to research how to provide the best care. The combination of easily accessible language, magical elements, and real scientific information (like how to conduct controlled experiments using the scientific method) makes these books an ideal introduction to basic STEM concepts.
More to Taste	**Kitchen Science Lab for Kids: 52 Family-Friendly Experiments from Around the House** by Liz Lee Heinecke **Olga and the Smelly Thing from Nowhere** by Elise Gravel **The Science Comics series** from Macmillan Publishers **The Boy Who Loved Math: The Improbable Life of Paul Erdos** by Deborah Heiligman

Fact-based

With all the meal-making, kid-transporting, and mess-cleaning that fill the typical parent's day, we often forget to step back and enjoy how fascinating the world around us can be. Information-filled books like these can help your kid experience the joy and wonder of discovering something new—and maybe help you recapture some of those feelings, too!

A Nibble

The Weird but True! books by National Geographic Kids
Our kids became obsessed with these books, always busting out the strangest facts at the most random times. Like the time we were reminding our littlest bookmonster about the snakes in glass cases we had seen at the zoo, and our middle bookmonster chimed in to inform us that snakes can't crawl across glass. Since the facts are so fascinating that they almost always leave you wanting more, the books are a powerful springboard for conversations and internet searches.

A Gobble

The Atlas Obscura Explorer's Guide for the World's Most Adventurous Kid by Dylan Thuras and Rosemary Mosco
This big, beautiful book features a collection of locations in the United States and elsewhere for your child to learn about. With elaborate illustrations and fun facts about each place, it will fascinate family members of all ages!

More to Taste

Botanicum: Welcome to the Museum by Katie Scott and Kathy Willis
Moon! Earth's Best Friend by Stacy McAnulty
National Geographic Kids Little Kids First Big Book of Dinosaurs by Catherine D. Hughes
What If You Had Animal Teeth? by Sandra Markle

Historical

Whether they're fully accurate accounts of historical events, or make-believe stories based on actual people's lives, books based on real things can be *really* interesting to your bookmonster!

A Nibble

Flush!: The Scoop on Poop Throughout the Ages by Charise Mericle Harper
Poop has never been more fun . . . or educational! This poetry-packed history lesson about all things potty is chock-full of fascinating facts.

A Gobble

Nurse, Soldier, Spy: The Story of Sarah Edmonds, a Civil War Hero
by Marissa Moss and John Hendrix
This book about Sarah Edmonds, a woman who disguised herself as a man to enlist as a soldier in the Civil War, is short enough to read in one sitting, but bursting with twists, turns, and intrigue.

More to Taste

The I Survived series by Lauren Tarshis
Let's Explore a Pirate Ship by Nicholas Harris
The Lives of . . . series by Kathleen Krull and Kathryn Hewitt
Ordinary, Extraordinary Jane Austen by Deborah Hopkinson
The Ordinary People Change the World series by Brad Meltzer

Activity books

These books are filled with puzzles, games, searches, and fill-in-the-blanks that encourage your kid to interact with what they're reading!

A Nibble

Where's Waldo? by Martin Handford
Search-and-find books are great introductory activity books, because they don't require reading skills and kids can enjoy them both with you and on their own.

A Gobble

Ivy + Bean + Me: A Fill-in-the-Blank Book by Annie Barrows
Full of prompts that kids can fill in with answers about their own opinions and experiences, books like these are fun now, and keepsakes later. After our eldest child completed this book, she loved looking back to rediscover her responses. If it's that fun to return to after only a couple of years, we're thinking it's going to seem even more endearing with age!

More to Taste

Big Magic for Little Hands by Joshua Jay
Don't Let the Pigeon Finish This Activity Book! by Mo Willems
Easy Origami by John Montroll
Mad Libs from Penguin Random House
Yoga for Kids by Susannah Hoffman

Storybooks

When most people think of "children's books," this is the category that comes to mind first. And because it's true that good ol' fiction books will likely fill up much of your child's bookshelf space, we gave this group one of the biggest sections in our bookmonster food pyramid. Your bookmonster will undoubtedly fall in love with countless books over the years, but they'll always remember their first loves . . . and that's exactly what we're talking about here.

The best stories contain fascinating characters, incredible events, and powerful emotions that engage us on a deeply human level. They can capture bookmonsters' imaginations by transporting them to far-away fantastical worlds, or bringing them to a better understanding of events that happen in their own lives. These are the books that your toddler will beg you to read first thing in the morning, and that your middle schooler will stay up late reading because they're just too exciting to put down. Because this group is so powerful, enjoyable, and rewarding, you'll definitely want to make sure to explore all the different types of stories you can!

Illustration-driven

They say a picture is worth a thousand words. So books that let pictures do the storytelling have a whole lot to say.

A Nibble	***Miss Sadie McGee Who Lived in a Tree*** written by Mark Kimball Moulton and illustrated by Karen Hillard Good The pictures in this book add tremendously to the story in their intricate charm, expansive foldout illustrations, and holes that provide peeks to images on successive pages.

A Gobble

Roller Girl by Victoria Jamieson
This fun read about a girl who decides to try the smashmouth sport of roller derby will inspire your family to try it, too (or at least to skate around for a couple non-violent laps)! We know sometimes adults frown on graphic novels, insisting that kids read "real books" instead. But we're all for anything that keeps our kiddos reading—so we say bring them on!

More to Taste

Because written by Mo Willems and illustrated by Amber Ren
The Bad Guys series by Aaron Blabey
The Bear's Song by Benjamin Chaud
The Mitten by Jan Brett

Text-driven

Even though lots of children's books rely heavily on illustrations, not all do. Reading books without explicit visuals or with a limited number of pictures in them can exercise kids' imaginations and focus their attention on the power of words.

A Nibble

The Book with No Pictures by B. J. Novak
Show your kiddo how entertaining words can be with this children's book that contains tons of fun despite not including a single picture.

A Gobble

Doctor Proctor's Fart Powder by Jo Nesbø
There are a few stylishly illustrated pics in this book, but with so much hilarious action packed into the words, your kid probably won't even need them.

More to Taste

Click, Clack, Moo: Cows that Type by Doreen Cronin
Sideways Stories from Wayside School by Louis Sachar
The Land of Stories series by Chris Colfer

Major life events

You can strategically use books that deal with emotions, milestones, and difficult issues like potty training, the birth of a sibling, transitioning to a big kid bed, the first day of school, moving to a new home, divorce, the death of a loved one, and more to help your little bookmonster when they encounter major life events of their own.

A Nibble

Princess of the Potty by Nora Gaydos
One of the most important things we did to prepare our kids for potty training was to read about it. Of the many, many, many potty books we read, this one was such a favorite for our littlest bookmonster that she was still asking us to read it months after she was potty trained!

A Gobble

Waiting for Baby by Harriet Ziefert
Getting a new sibling is a huge transition, and reading books about it ahead of time provides the perfect opportunity to emotionally prepare kids for the important role they'll have as an older sibling. This book emphasizes how happy the main character is to meet the new baby, and how very hard it is to wait for something so exciting!

More to Taste

Because of Winn-Dixie by Kate DiCamillo
How Do You Feel? by Anthony Browne
I'm Not Moving! by Wiley Blevins
The Best of Both Nests by Jane Clarke

Extended read-alouds

In addition to enjoying shorter reads throughout the day, we encourage you to pick a longer, more advanced book that your bookmonster is interested in, and then read it aloud together over an extended time. Opening up a book you've been sharing for days or weeks is like watching an episode of your favorite show—you already know and love the characters and you're excited to find out what happens next. Even kids as young as preschool age can enjoy extended read-alouds, especially if you remind them of what's happened in the story so far before starting each reading session, and help translate confusing plot twists and new vocabulary.

A Nibble	***Big Foot and Little Foot*** by Ellen Potter This book is long enough to separate across multiple reading sessions, but the numerous illustrations and fairly simple story about a sasquatch becoming unlikely friends with a boy makes it a great early read-aloud.
A Gobble	**The Snoop Troop series** by Kirk Scroggs This book is ideal for early chapter book readers to consume on their own, and even more fun to enjoy as a group! Readers follow a boy and girl mystery-solving duo as they tackle some of the most pressing cases the city has ever seen—like who put stink bugs in the cafeteria's sloppy joes? With funny plot twists, seek-and-find pictures, and clues for the reader to decode along the way, it's fun from beginning to end!
More to Taste	***Gangsta Granny*** by David Walliams **The Chronicles of Narnia series** by C. S. Lewis ***The Indian in the Cupboard*** by Lynne Reid Banks ***The Neddiad*** by Daniel Pinkwater

Unique interests

And now we've reached the final group of books that make up any bookmonster's healthy and complete diet. You'll see that it's the biggest category in the Book Pyramid, and that all the other types of books rest on top of it. That's because it is incredibly important—in fact, you can't raise a bookmonster without it. This group is different for every bookmonster out there, and could contain literally any type of book you might think of, including those that fall into each of the categories above it. The only requirement for a book belonging to this group is that your individually unique bookmonster finds it *interesting*!

That's the whole point of raising a bookmonster, after all. You don't merely want your child to meet the bare minimum requirements of learning how to read. You also want them to learn to love reading. The best way to do that is by making sure they understand that the things they're most interested in can be found, explored, and enjoyed in books. Think about the ever-changing list of things your child is into, and look for books that bring those topics to life. The times when your child becomes wildly, unpredictably, and utterly obsessed with a particular topic—like doctors, unicorns, fairies, babies, or pie—are perfect times to head to the library. Once kids realize that their unique interests can always align with reading, they will choose to do it often, and get better and better at it as they do.

A Nibble	*Say "Ahhh!": Dora Goes to the Doctor* by Phoebe Beinstein What our doctor-obsessed daughter liked most about this book were the descriptions of particular medical tools and what they're used for. She even begged us to get her real versions of the tools for her birthday!
A Gobble	**The Notebook of Doom series** by Troy Cummings This series was perfect for our son's long-term and wide-ranging monster obsession, since each of its many books focuses on a different totally inventive monster. With fun stories and lots of illustrations, it's also a great way for little ones to ease into reading chapter books independently.
More to Taste	*Be a Star, Wonder Woman* by Michael Dahl *Artist Ted* by Andrea Beaty *Not Quite Narwhal* by Jessie Sima *Thelma the Unicorn* by Aaron Blabey *The Monsterator* by Keith Graves

Laying Off the Reading Levels

Although many schools find it useful to assign books of particular levels to entire classrooms full of kids, we urge you not to limit your bookmonster at home in a similar way. Restricting children's book choices can have the unintended effect of restricting their interest in reading as well. And because bookmonsters are constantly exploring and learning, they can benefit from exposure to all kinds of books—above or below arbitrary age designations.

If kids want to read books above their grade levels, we say let them! They might surprise you and be able to understand everything just fine, and if they don't, you can be there to help them through hard parts. Likewise, if they want to check out a book that someone says is only for younger kids, who cares? Reading something is better than reading nothing. As long as they're choosing to read and enjoying the experience, it's a positive thing.

Some of our family's favorite reading memories have come about because we bucked arbitrary age recommendations. Our earliest days as parents included reading books to the baby that people would consider both appropriate (simple picture books like *Goodnight Moon* by Margaret Wise Brown) as well as too advanced (more intricate and elaborate books like *Goldilocks and the Three Bears* as retold by Jim Aylesworth). Although our newborn couldn't yet understand the words or plot, she would lie next to us with her eyes fixed on the book, kicking with excitement as she listened to our voices.

Kids can benefit from books far below their designated reading levels as well. Even after our two oldest bookmonsters could read chapter books on their own, they still occasionally liked to sit and listen to us read basic picture books to their baby sister. Although you might assume that they wouldn't get much from such a reading, they sure enjoyed the rewarding experience of a great group cuddle and a reunion with one of their past favorite books.

14

Speaking a Bookmonster's Language

C ows go moo. Pigs go oink. Sheep go baa. And roosters go cock-a-doodle-doo. But what sounds do bookmonsters make? Do these wild, rambunctious creatures roar, grunt, or maybe even growl? Nope! The noises a bookmonster loves to make most are all related to language. We're talking about things like:

- saying letter names and sounds
- rhyming
- alliterating
- breaking words into individual sounds
- blending letter sounds together

What these skills have in common is that they're all ways for children to demonstrate their developing *phonological awareness*—or ability to recognize the sounds of language. When kids notice that words like "hot" and "pot" rhyme, for instance, they are showing understanding that the end of each word sounds the same. When they can identify that "stop," "skip," and "soup" all start with the same letter, they are demonstrating awareness that the beginning of the words sound the same. And when they run around the house yelling "hot pot poop soup, hot pot poop soup," they are reminding you that you're waaaaay overdue for a kid-free date night.

Research shows that phonological awareness is one of the two most important skills children need to learn how to read. (Amassing a large vocabulary is the other one, by the way.) It's crucial that children learn this stuff, and unlike many of the tips you've read in this book already, getting your kid to understand how language and letter sounds work is going to require some direct coaching from you.

If you're panicking right now because you thought you weren't going to have to do any teaching at all here, and this sounds a lot like teaching to you, and you are definitely not ready for this, and you have no idea how to even make your rug rat remember to wash hands after going to the bathroom, much less absorb your instruction on this highly technical-sounding phonological awareness insanity . . . relax! Believe it or not, you already know how to teach your kid plenty of stuff. (How else did they learn the moo, oink, baa, and cock-a-doodle-doo sounds all those barnyard animals make?) Besides, nothing we're about to show you needs to feel like a tedious lesson for your child, or for you. Just remember to approach practicing phonological skills the same way you approach shared reading. Talk, laugh, smile, and if it stops being fun, then do something else. All bookmonsters learn to read at their own pace, so there's no need to push educational concepts like these too hard or too early. Instead, simply sprinkle in some natural instruction while you're having fun together, and you'll be just fine!

Saying letter names and sounds

Learning the names of the letters and the sounds they make is an absolute must for every future reader. That's why elementary school teachers who are focused on helping students build foundational skills for reading emphasize them so much. But don't just leave letter lessons to your kid's classroom. Children can begin to understand educational concepts earlier than you might think. And their skills will develop sooner when parents introduce and support them at home— regardless of a child's age or grade level.

How exactly should you do that? Well, in addition to frequently singing the good ol' alphabet song, here are some more ideas:

Play with letter toys

It's a good idea to invest in some basic alphabet toys like letter puzzles and refrigerator magnets that you can use frequently. Try to focus your talk around concepts that are just beyond what your bookmonster already knows. For example, if you're pretty sure that your bookmonster already knows the letters A, B, and C, steer the conversation toward the letter D and beyond. You'll find that your conversations will naturally get more sophisticated over time, lining up with your child's increasing skill.

Talk about letters when reading

When you read to your kid, pause the story every once in a while and comment about the letters and words on the page. Prominently displayed words like the book's title, or text that appears in one of the book's pictures, are easy places to start. For example, you can touch each word in a book's title as you read it, describing how you know which word is which by looking at their first letters. For *Go, Dog. Go!* by P. D. Eastman, say, "I can tell that the first and last word are "Go" because G sounds like *guh*, and the middle word must be "Dog" because D sounds like *duh*!" During future reading sessions you can naturally extend conversations like this by sounding out all of the letters in the words to model reading the entire title, asking which word is which in the title, and eventually asking your kid to read the title to you.

Talk about letters in other ways, too

When we started introducing letters to our bookmonsters, we realized that we were almost exclusively showing them uppercase letters. But that's only part of the story. Expand your exchanges to include the following aspects of letters:

- **Lowercase letters.** Since most books contain lots more lowercase than uppercase letters, kids need to learn those as well. Look for letter puzzles and toys that include both uppercase and lowercase letters so you'll easily be able to incorporate them into conversations while you play. *The Sleepy Little Alphabet* by Judy Sierra features lowercase letters playfully illustrated as little kid versions of their big uppercase parents. This way of thinking about letters was a perfect fit for our family, since we found it useful to use the relatable terms "mommy and daddy" letters and "baby" letters when our kids first started learning the alphabet. While kids will eventually need to know the proper terms, this kind of parental pairing shows that uppercase and lowercase letters belong together and are bigger and smaller versions of the same thing— even if they sometimes look very different from one another.

- **Letter sounds.** When you think about it, knowing the sound a letter makes is far more important than knowing what the letter is named. That's why we taught our kids both letter names and sounds at the same time—using the associated sound as often as possible whenever we mentioned a letter. As our child fit each letter into a puzzle, for instance, we would say, "That's a *B*. It says buh, buh." We also frequently extended this information by discussing examples of words that start with each letter, and then asking the kids to think of more. Since knowing letter sounds is so important in determining children's success at learning how to read, you might as well bring them up as often as possible.

- **Letter combinations.** At some point, after you've done a lot of talking about letter sounds and practicing sounding out words, you'll discover that just knowing the sounds that individual letters make isn't enough. Some letter combinations like ph, ch, sh, th, and oo make sounds that are just too unexpected, so you'll need to tell your kid about them specifically when you encounter them in text. Just like with single letters, ask your kid to help you come up with words that include combinations, and challenge them to figure out which combinations are included in words you think up.

Rhyming

Experience with the kinds of rhymes found in ordinary children's books can lead to extraordinary reading and spelling skills. Researchers back in the 1980s established a strong connection between familiarity with nursery rhymes and reading, showing that kids who knew more nursery rhymes at age three were better readers at age six.

Was there something particularly educational about the exploits of Jack, Jill, and some old lady who lived in a shoe? Probably not, as the reading benefits are linked less to specific content, and more to the rhyming nature of the poems. Which is quite a relief, since people tend to read fewer nursery rhymes nowadays, plus a lot of them are woefully outdated. Like, how many girls should Georgie Porgie be able to kiss and make cry before someone teaches him the meaning of consent? And why is Peter Peter Pumpkin Eater allowed to keep his wife in a pumpkin shell anyway? If you're interested in reading more of these bizarre, antiquated oddities, check out an anthology like *The Original Mother Goose* illustrated by Blanche Fisher Wright.

And if you're interested in helping your child tune in to the sounds of language by increasing rhyme time in your home, try these ideas:

Read rhyming books

Lots of great children's books rhyme, like *The Goodnight Train* by June Sobel—and every single Dr. Seuss story ever written. Kids will learn important lessons about language sounds simply by listening to you read books like these.

Sing rhyming songs

Many classic children's songs rhyme, like "The Itsy Bitsy Spider," "Twinkle, Twinkle, Little Star," "Head, Shoulders, Knees and Toes," and tons of others. Rhyming songs can be repeated over and over again, giving kids the chance to consider the rhyming elements over time.

Play with puppets

Pretend that a puppet or stuffed animal has a rhymable name and think of some words that rhyme with it. Early on, you can generate rhyming words together: "This is Joe. He likes words that rhyme with his name, like 'no' and 'go.' Let's think of some words and see if he would like them!" When your child gets the hang of rhyming, you can make identifying the correct rhyming word into a game: "Which word would Joe like better: 'slow' or 'pan'?"

Have a scavenger hunt

Go on a rhyming scavenger hunt around your home! Initially, you can walk around and find things that rhyme together. Once your kid's able to do it without you, you can add a relay element by challenging them to bring back a pair of objects that rhyme as fast as they can. Ready, set? You bet!

Spit some rhymes

Write your own songs, spoken-word poems, or rap lyrics—then perform them together! It'll give kids a truly memorable rhyming lesson, and parents an excuse to bust out their old-school beatboxing skillz.

Alliterating

Words that start with the same letter sounds alliterate, as in "temper tantrum," "stop screaming," and "clean this colossal collection of clutter, kids!" When you hear alliteration (or assonance, which is the repetition of vowel sounds rather than consonant sounds), you can totally tell. Here are some ideas about how to bring more alliteration to your bunch:

Try talking about it

An easy place to start involves simply pointing out words that share the same first letter sound when you're reading or chatting. "*Family* starts with *F*, just like *fun!*"

Assign alliterative names

Make funny nicknames for each other, friends, stuffed animals, and anyone else you can think of by alliterating or assonating their names with another word. It's a great way to boost kids' spelling skills and self-esteem. (At least "Awesome" Amber and "Amazing" Andy think so!)

Make silly sentences

Take turns coming up with alliterative sentences that follow a pattern, like: "__(Name)__ the __(Animal)__ loves to eat __(Food)__." See if you can fill in the blanks all the way from Arnold Alpaca eating anchovies to Zoe Zebra eating zucchini. The silly sentences can match any form you like. Our kids like to have fun with one based on the first letters of each of the planets, as in "Magical mustaches playing maracas on Mars."

Breaking words into individual sounds

Learning to break words into their smaller, separate sounds is a central precursor to learning how to read. And the better kids get at it, the faster they'll start flipping pages on their own.

Most kids follow a fairly predictable progression in developing the ability to work with increasingly smaller and subtler sound units. First, they figure out how to break words up into larger chunks like syllables. Next, they can isolate the more obvious first and last letter sounds of the word—although this gets trickier when the sounds are clustered with other consonants. For example, it's easier to name *F* as the first sound in *fish*, and harder to identify it in *frog*. Finally, children who are most ready to read become able to divide words into each of their individual letter sounds.

Once you know roughly what to expect as your bookmonster learns to break up words, you can anticipate these milestones and target your conversations toward what's coming next. In addition to simply talking about how you can break up letter sounds, here are some fun activities that will give your bookmonster some practice:

Clap out syllables

Clapping while you talk isn't just for adding seriously snarky emphasis to social media comments. It's also an entertainingly interactive way to introduce your kid to separating sounds. Just pick a word, and clap once as you say each syl-la-ble. "Check it out: I clapped three times, which means *syllable* has three syllables. What word do you want to try clapping out?"

Tap out letter sounds

Once your child has gotten comfortable with clapping syllables, try tapping out individual letter sounds. To make tapping practice feel like a game, gather a bunch of household objects and toys with names that are three letters long and follow a simple consonant-vowel-consonant construction (like cup, pot, hat and pig). Next, draw three circles on a piece of paper in a horizontal row. Model how you can tap each circle once from left to right as you say the individual sounds in each three-letter word. So for the pig, you'd place it in front of you and tap the left circle while saying *puh*, the middle circle while saying *ih*, and the right circle while saying *guh*. Then say the sounds together as the whole word "pig" while running your hand across the circles from left to right. Encourage your child to try it out next. If they don't yet understand what you mean by tapping once for each sound, encourage them to tap while they say "just a little bit" of the word at a time. With practice and increasing letter experience, they'll soon get the *huh, aa, n, guh* of it.

Figure out what's left

Challenge each other to omit sounds from words, as in, "Say the word *top*. Now say it again but leave out the *tuh* sound." If that's too tricky at first, it might be easier to use compound words ("*Batman* without the *bat*") or syllables ("*doctor* without the *doc*"). You can add a little mystery to this basic letter omission activity by taking out sounds that result in new real words for your kid to figure out. For example, challenge them to figure out which real word is left when you remove the *luh* sound from *slit*, or the *buh* sound from *band*, or the *nuh* sound from *pent*. We could go on and on—and so can you!

Go round and round with sounds

This cool game (which our kids taught *us* one day) requires you to think about both the beginnings and the endings of words, all at the same time. The first person picks any word they want (like "alligator"). The next person has to come up with a new word that begins with the last sound from the first word (so "alligator" can lead to "origami"). The person after that does it again (with "origami" leading to "meteor"), and on and on, as long as you can keep the word inspiration going!

Blending letter sounds together

Of all the phonological awareness activities, blending letter sounds has the most obvious connection to reading. Hearing your child do it will be an exciting glimpse into their reading future, and once kids get the hang of looking at a row of letters, identifying their individual sounds, and smushing all those sounds together, reading is exactly what they really will be doing!

Write words wherever

Sprinkle in quick sound-blending practice sessions here and there during your normal everyday activities by writing words on whatever's handy—a chalkboard, one of those magnetic drawing pads that erase when you slide that thingy across the bottom, your computer, a napkin, a sandbox, the dirt, or anything else that you can fit a few letters on. Write a word and ask your kid to try sounding out the letters and blending them together. (Or, in other words, practice reading them!) Keeping these little quizzes brief and playful means they'll never seem like work.

Practice your ABZs

While you're writing a word, show how you can swap out one of the letters to magically transform it into a whole new word. Like, after your child has blended sounds to figure out what the word "top" says, write the word "tot" underneath it. Challenge your kiddo to figure out the new word, and then point out that because only the very last letter is different, it means that "top" and "tot" start the same. (Also, you're a "top tot" for reading these words so well!) You can do the same activity by switching first letters (making "map" into "nap") or middle letters (turning "zap" into "zip").

Bring in a blend-a-bear

Introduce your bookmonster to a new teddy bear or other stuffed animal, and explain that this toy speaks in a unique way. "This bear can only speak in *sounds*, and we need to try to figure out what she's trying to say." Then bust out your best puppet voice and have the stuffed animal say words separated into their individual sounds, like "Huh. I!" Make sure you pause between each letter sound you make, and give your kid a chance to realize this new friend is saying the word "Hi!" You can help by gradually saying the sounds closer together, and even connecting the sounds yourself if your child doesn't figure it out fairly soon. If you do it together and offer support during the task, your kid will be less likely to get frustrated or give up, even as words get longer or trickier. Try this with lots and lots of words, and over time your bookmonster will learn to understand your "blend-a-bear" with ease!

Do a little dance

The "tap and sweep" sound blending activity lets kids release a little energy while learning literacy lessons. In this exercise, bookmonsters use their favored hand to tap the sounds of a word along their opposite arm, with the first sound on their shoulder, the second sound on their elbow, and the third sound on their wrist. Then they sweep it all the way down their arm from top to bottom while they blend the sounds together. To tap and sweep the word "dip" for example, kids would tap their shoulders while they make the *D* sound, tap their elbows while they make the *I* sound, tap their wrists while they make the *P* sound, and then slide their hands smoothly from shoulder to elbow to wrist as they say "dip" all together. Get the whole family on their feet to tap and sweep together!

Music to a Bookmonster's Ears

Did you know that playing and listening to music activates the same brain regions that are used to process language sounds and patterns? So give your bookmonster's brain a workout by playing your favorite songs when the family's at home or in the car, and getting your kid some basic musical instruments like a drum, harmonica, recorder, tambourine, and xylophone.

If you happen to have musical skills yourself, we encourage you to share them with your child. Andy started teaching each of our littles how to play the piano when they were about four years old, and he and the kids cherish the time they spend making music together. Besides being a fun way for them to express themselves, formal musical training also teaches kids more advanced lessons about how language works. Reading and playing sheet music requires learning how to decipher odd-looking symbols and translate them into sounds you can create and hear—just like reading all those odd-looking letter symbols in a book and using them to say words and sentences that make sense. When children learn to play a musical instrument, they're not just learning how to make beautiful noises that are fun to listen to—they're also building a basic understanding of symbols that will help them learn to read!

15

Working a Bookmonster's Memory

They say that elephants never forget. Bottlenose dolphins will recognize each other's calls after two decades apart. And Clark's nutcrackers can store twenty thousand different seed-burying locations in their bird brains. But none of these creatures' memories can compete with that of the bookmonster. And with a seed-sized bit of memory training, your bookmonster can grow some elephant-sized reading skills.

What role does memory play in reading? It's a good question, and one that even literacy experts haven't always agreed upon. For years, an intense debate raged about how to best teach children to read. Should kids be taught the phonics method of sounding out the individual letters that make up words, or should they be guided to memorize whole words as a single unit? It was a smackdown of epic proportions with winner-take-all stakes, as many people believed that the two approaches could not possibly coexist. Teachers were entrenched in camps that either taught endless phonics drills or tasked kids with increasingly long lists of words to commit to memory whole. This became known as the "Reading Wars," and after ages of combat and carnage, one clear loser emerged: the kids.

Since then, a tremendous amount of research has shown that everybody in the Reading Wars was right . . . and wrong. In other words, there's a time and place to use *both* approaches. We now know that instructing children in letters and letter sounds is absolutely essential, as it's the only way to equip kids to deal with words they haven't already been trained to read. For example, kids may be taught to identify the word "snow," but memorizing that word wouldn't necessarily help them identify similar words like "grow" or "snap"—unless they are *also* instructed in individual letter sounds and combinations. Even we adults who can read fluently sometimes rely on sounding out letters when we first encounter new words in text.

Sight words are super powerful

The problem with sounding out every single word every time you see it? It's an incredibly inefficient way to read. That's why bookmonsters know that some words are better consumed *whole*. Learning to read frequently repeated words by memorizing them is an effective strategy that can lead to speedy short-term gains. Children can go from not being able to read any words at all to recognizing a whole bunch of words that they've memorized in a very short time—and that kind of success can be incredibly motivating!

These words are often called "sight words," because children can be coached to identify them on sight, quickly and easily recognizing them in text. Here's a starter list of some commonly coached sight words:

a/an	have	of	want
and	help	play	was
are	here	said	we
can	I	see	what
come	is	she/he	where
do/does	like	that	who
for	little	the	with
go	look	they	you
good	me	this	
has	my	to/too	

Encourage your kid to memorize as many of these as you see useful until they're capable of reading the words on their own. In our house, we tend to emphasize a few of the most frequently occurring sight words without worrying too much about covering the entire exhaustive list. But you should do whatever seems to work best with your bookmonster.

Memorizing more than words

Another reason your bookmonster may need to rely on memorization is that written words aren't completely predictable. The English language can be particularly bonkers to read, with many letters making different sounds in different words. So in addition to memorizing whole words, it will be necessary for your bookmonster to memorize some specific rules—like that an *e* at the end of a word is often "magic," because it is silent and makes the vowel before it say its own name.

Your child will also want to memorize how particular groups of letters sound together. Try to sound out the individual sounds in common letter groupings like "ar," "ing," and "tion" and you'll see what we mean. Many letter combinations sound nothing like the sum of their individual sounds. That's why typical word endings, prefixes, suffixes, and vowel combinations are often taught as "sight chunks." Teach your child to recognize that common letter combinations behave as single units, and they'll be able to quickly pronounce them when they appear in words. Here's a list of some useful sight chunks:

ai (pair)	ed (skipped)	ing (sing)	oy (toy)
ar (car)	ee (bee)	oa (boat)	sh (shoe)
aw (saw)	er (soccer)	oo (toot)	th (this)
ay (play)	ew (new)	or (for)	tion (potion)
ch (chocolate)	ie (movie)	ou (sour)	wh (what)
ea (meat)	igh (night)	ow (cow)	

One easy way to teach your kid to memorize words and chunks is to talk about them as part of the discussions you have during everyday book reading. When our bookmonsters were first beginning to try to sound out words and they came to a sight word like "said," we would remind them: "That's a memorize word—it's *said*," or "Remember that memorize word?" Sight chunks can be addressed in a similar way. When children are beginning to sound out words and they come to a sight chunk like "er," you can give them an explicit reminder like: "Remember, *e r* says *errr*." This communicates to your kid that they should pay attention to remembering the whole word or chunk as a unit and not bother with sounding out the individual letters. The more practice kids get encountering the words and chunks in text, the easier it gets to remember them.

A menu of memory-building games

Here are some additional activities that can get your bookmonster gobbling up sight words and chunks in no time:

Sight word sprint

Write sight words or chunks on pieces of paper and scatter them on the floor. Shout out one of the words or chunks and have your bookmonster run to the corresponding card as fast as they can.

Sight word hide-and-seek

Dust off your old, long-forgotten drinking game supplies, because this game requires some disposable cups and a ping pong ball. Flip the cups over and write a sight word or chunk on each one. Then hide the ball under one of the cups, and challenge your bookmonster to find it by correctly identifying the sight word or chunk that it's under: "Can you find the ball under *for*?"

Sight word art show

Gather up some art supplies you think your kid could get really into, like finger paints, stamps, bingo daubers, sidewalk chalk, or giant cans of whipped cream. Write a bunch of sight words or chunks on a surface you don't mind getting messy, like pieces of cardboard or the driveway. Then call out one of the sight words or chunks, and let your baby-faced Banksy graffiti it!

Sight word scavenger hunt

Write down a list of sight words or chunks twice—once on a piece of paper, and once on sticky notes that you hide all around the house. Send your kid off to find as many words as possible, returning to stick them onto the corresponding words or chunks on the list. Bonus for you: While your kid is off looking, you'll get a precious few moments to set *your* sights on a cup of coffee, a book that was written for adults, or the back of your own eyelids!

16

The Magic of a Bookmonster's Name

The names we give to animals serve many different purposes. They can describe how a species looks, like the naked mole rat's name certainly does. They can let creatures know we're talking to them, like they do when we're calling for our pets. And in the case of bookmonsters, they can do the most powerful thing of all—motivate little kids to develop a massive interest in reading!

Wondering how this might work? It's simple, really. Your name is an incredibly special word to you throughout life, starting from your very earliest days. At four months old, infants already recognize the sound of their own name. And because that special word so often comes from the lips of parents, older siblings, and other sources of love, a child's name is set up to feel like a warm, reassuring blanket that's always ready for a snuggle.

This helps explain why, as we get older, we tend to be drawn to people and things that have names similar to ours. That's right—whether you know it or not, you've likely been increasing your opinion of stuff if its name shares letters with yours. We know we've done it. Amber orders *amber* beers much more often than blondes or browns. Andy would probably say *Andy Kaufman* is his favorite comedian of all time. And it turns out that this effect is so strong, people end up dispro-portionately marrying people whose names resemble their own. So perhaps it wasn't just by chance that *Amber N. Aguiar* married *Andrew M. Ankowski* and eventually made a house full of bookmonsters.

Start with the first letter

Since names are so naturally interesting and influential, you can use them to get your child excited about things like spelling, reading, and writing—even if they haven't shown much interest in those activities before. Studies observing the way parents and kids talk about letters show that conversations last significantly longer and result in more child participation when they include talk about the first letter in the child's name. That's pretty cool, right? If little Penelope is yawning her way through your lecture on how *apple* starts with *a*, she'll probably perk right up if you switch gears and tell her that *pear* starts with *p* . . . just like her name! Talking about your bookmonster's name makes al-phabet discussions more personal, way more interesting, and way, way more beneficial for building literacy skills. So much so that researchers have found that kids whose parents use their names to inspire interac-tions about letters when they're three and four years old have better reading skills at the end of kindergarten.

Once kids realize the letter that starts their first name is their *very own letter*, they will delight in finding it everywhere. They'll be inter-ested to discover the sound it makes and words that have the same first letter in common, including which animals, foods, and other people they suddenly share something very special with. So when you're talking about the alphabet, be sure to make a big, huge, how-freaking-cool-is-this deal about your child's special letter!

Names, names everywhere

After you've hooked your kiddo on that first letter, move on to foster a zest for the rest. And don't stop there, because bookmonsters will enjoy rhyming, alliterating, and playing all sorts of language games with their names. Here are some specific ideas about how to help your kid go nuts for their name:

Sing "The Name Game"

If you're like us, you sang this oldie a lot when you were a kid. Well, now it's time to share it with the next generation. Just pick a name, and throw it into these lyrics: *Daddy daddy bo-baddy, banana fanna fo-faddy, fee fie mo maddy, Daddy!* But think ahead if you're concerned about what words you might end up singing in front of your child. (We're looking at you, Art!)

Try some name navigating

When you're in the car, play the Alphabet Game from the "Bookmonsters on the Loose" chapter (page 85), but instead of finding all the letters from A to Z on the signs, cars, and buildings you pass, search for the letters that spell your bookmonster's name instead. If the game ends too quickly because you named your kid something short like DJ, do it with middle and last names, too. It'll help kids learn their full names and get them familiar with even more letters!

Read books that include your kid's name

Lots of children's books feature character names prominently, some-times right on the cover. If you can find one with your bookmonster's name on it, it's sure to pique some serious interest. We own at least one book with each of our kids' names in the title, and they absolutely *love* them. Even if these books don't contain the most amazing story you've ever read, your bookmonster will still relish imagining them-selves as one of the characters! And these days, if you can't find a book with your child's name in the title, a quick internet search will reveal multiple companies that let you order one custom-made.

Label lots and lots

The more children see letters and words, the more familiar and com-fortable with them they'll become. So if you're going to buy something for your child anyway, like a lunchbox, T-shirt, decorative pillow, or wall decoration, you might as well see if there's a personalized version of it available. One of the coolest items we picked up for our kids were stepstools with their names on them. Since stepstools empower shorties to be more self-sufficient—reaching toys, the sink, or Mom-my's phone, darn it—positive feelings get paired with reading every time they take a step!

Write name lists

In case your child is among the 100 percent of children who occa-sionally have a teensy-weensy bit of trouble sharing, you might want to give this name-based solution a try. Instead of hollering over and over at the kids to take turns on the slide, you can write a quick list showing the order they get to go in. Kids will get more exposure to their names as they refer to the list to try to figure out who is who and when it's their turn. Plus, by putting it down on paper, you've some-how made it more official and worthy of your kid's respect.

Be a real artist

Professional artists don't just paint pictures and call it a day. They have to sign their names on their art first! Encourage your kid to sign the "masterpieces" they create with whatever squiggles, letters, names, or full-on signatures they're capable of. Amber's grandma—an avid painter who sometimes gives lessons to the kids—is awesome at this. After setting up our pint-size Picassos with canvases, paints, and tips for adding realism to their creations, she always hands them a marker to sign their names right in the corner—no matter how big or little they are.

Put your names to music

Our family loves to ~~butcher~~ modify songs to include all sorts of our own lyrics, and some of the biggest crowd favorites include ones that feature our kids' names. Classics like "You Are My Sunshine," "Twin-kle, Twinkle, Little Star," and "I've Been Working on the Railroad" have familiar tunes that are easy to maintain while swapping out a few key words. So give Dinah a break, and let someone be "in the kitchen with" your kid every once in a while.

Make a name puzzle

Store-bought letter puzzles like the ones mentioned in the "Speak-ing a Bookmonster's Language" chapter (page 146) are excellent for promoting spatial development, problem-solving, and early reading skills. To add a personal touch to this activity, try making homemade puzzles featuring words, phrases, or sentences that are special to your family—like your bookmonster's name! Find some sturdy card stock or cardboard, write your child's name on it and decorate it however you like, cut it up into puzzle-shaped pieces, and tell your kiddo to get to work!

Find your names in the credits

When our family goes out to the movies, we like to stick around for all the credits (and it's not just to see if there's some fun bonus footage at the very end). What we like best about it is scanning the scrolling text, looking for people who have the same first names as us. Anytime someone spots a family member's name in the credits, they shout and point so we can all find it. Sometimes, it's more exciting than the movie.

Names help with reading, and writing, too

Probably the most noteworthy name-related milestones in the lives of bookmonsters are when they learn to spell and write their own names—and you never know when kids will put the pieces together to start doing it. We were shocked one day when our son marched over to us holding a toy catalog he had gone through cover to cover, marking up page after page with all the new gear he wanted. The kid had never, *ever* written a single letter before then, and suddenly almost every single toy in the catalog was circled and marked with the first letter of his name. Apparently, all he needed to start writing his name was the proper motivation!

When events like that happen with your growing bookmonster, make sure you take a moment to truly celebrate them. Say how cool it is, and what great work they're doing reading and writing like a big kid! Don't worry that they form their letters all wonky, or that they're scattered all over the paper in no particular order right now. Kids will learn exactly how to write their names soon enough, and then they'll ask to borrow your car to go out on a date, and then they'll come visit you in your retirement home a couple times a month if you're lucky. We may have gotten off on a little tangent there, but the point is this: Enjoy every moment you have with your little one, don't forget to appreciate as many small steps along the way as possible, and take advantage of your child's name to promote positive feelings toward reading and writing whenever you can!

17

Bookmonsters Like Laughing

A goose can be silly. A hyena can laugh. And a barrel of monkeys can look pretty darn funny. Having a sense of humor is incredibly important to bookmonsters, too. Not only are jokes fun for everybody in the family, they're also frequently full of thought-provoking twists and wisecracking wordplay that can end up teaching your bookmonster loads of highly valuable language lessons.

Think we're joking? We're as serious as a fart attack.

While kids' jokes are undeniably silly (ours are too, apparently), they can be surprisingly smart as well. Take this little gem:

QUESTION: Why did the banana go to the doctor?
ANSWER: Because it wasn't peeling well!

Most adults who read that would probably see the play on words immediately, acknowledge that yes, in fact, the content and structure make this identifiable as a joke, and perhaps offer up a nod and polite half smile in response. Your kid, on the other hand, will enjoy the heck out of it—cracking up, repeating the punch line with glee, and filling the room with *peels* of laughter. (Get it?)

While they're having the time of their young life laughing at that produce-at-the-pediatrician gag, let's stop to think about everything your child had to understand to make this moment possible. First, they had to notice that you said something that was not correct (or at least out of the ordinary). Next, they had to know that you did so on purpose, instead of it just being an accidental slip of the tongue. Then, they had to realize that you did it to entertain them. And finally, they had to comprehend that the reason this unusual thing you intentionally said is entertaining is because people go to the doctor when they're not feeling well, bananas have peels, *feeling* and *peeling* rhyme with each other, and therefore the idea that bananas would go to the doctor when they're not peeling well is, in a word, *funny*.

We know that might seem like a whole lot of unnecessary analysis for a simple little joke. But it's important to realize that your child's brain is doing all that analysis, lightning-fast, every time a joke is told. Because jokes are such amazing mental workouts, it's no wonder studies have shown that children with more developed senses of humor score higher on tests of intelligence, creativity, language, and literacy.

Plus, everything's more fun when you add some jokes—having conversations over dinner, standing in line at the store, getting tucked into bed at night, and yes, learning how to read. Keep this in mind as you introduce books and language skill-building to your child. The more fun you have with it, the more interested your kiddo will be. And there's a good chance they'll end up learning more, too, as research shows that people tend to remember humorous lessons better than ultra-serious ones.

Are you sold on the benefits of humor, but concerned that you're just not that funny? Well, that's because you're not. (Just kidding. That was a joke. . . . Unless you're actually not funny, in which case it was merely an insightful bit of commentary.) But here's the thing: You don't need a tight twenty-minute stand-up routine showcasing your unique brand of esoteric observational humor to tell your child a couple of gags. Kids' jokes are formulaic, rarely require any kind of skilled timing or delivery, and are easily accessible by an online search or trip to your local library's Humor section. And kids are an easy audience anyway, so they're bound to love the jokes you tell them no matter what. We know because Amber is just about the worst tickler in the entire world, but somehow our kids still giggle with glee whenever she wags her objectively inept tickle fingers anywhere near them. Your kid is sure to do the same as soon as you start tickling some funny bones!

Here are some ideas for getting your bookmonster guffawing at every age.

Ages 0 and up

Before your bookmonster is about two years old, physical comedy will be your best bet for laughs. Go for anything that is overt, action-based, and makes you look totally ridiculous. Stand on your head, eat grapes out of your armpit, and cluck around like a chicken.

You'll be surprised by how early infants can respond to comedy—and even make some of their own! As young as five months old, infants already find absurd events funny. By eight months old, babies can create their own jokes by making silly faces or noises, starting to hand you something and then snatching it away, pretending to snore, or creating their own outrageous actions like putting shoes on their hands.

A major reason kids find slapstick shenanigans so funny (and not utterly frightening) is that you tend to have a great big grin on your face the entire time you're clowning around. And because kids are inherently social, they're able to read your expressions of happiness and laughter, pay attention to the kinds of things that create your glee, and develop a sense of humor themselves.

Ages 2 and up

By the time kids are two, they've already built some serious language skills. Even if they're not talking a lot, they can understand much of the language they hear, which means verbal jokes can begin generating lots of laughs. They may even begin to produce their own—which is extra fun!

Some of the easiest jokes for younger talkers to tackle are basically *lies*. Try coaxing out some chuckles by saying things that the whole family *knows* aren't true:

- "Isn't the sky a lovely shade of green today?"
- "Dinner's canceled because an abominable snowman ate everything in our kitchen."
- "Tonight you get to tuck your parents into bed instead!"

Ages 3 and up

When kids are three years old, they can really begin to appreciate the sounds of language, aka phonological awareness, which we covered in the "Speaking a Bookmonster's Language" chapter (page 146). Thanks to this new attentiveness to sounds, children learn that some words rhyme—and that replacing a word with one of its rhymes is *hilarious*. Which brings a whole new category of jokes for the family to share. "Pass the spaghetti and feetballs, please!"

Sharing simple, formulaic wisecracks like knock-knock jokes around this age can help your youngster begin to recognize what a joke typically sounds like—and start making some of their own. You know how these gags go: "Knock-knock." "Who's there?" "Lena." "Lena who?" "Lena little closer and I'll tell you another joke!"

Ages 4 and up

As children's language skills develop even further, they'll begin to appreciate more nuanced aspects of words, and jokes that play around with them. Now homonyms, synonyms, and words with multiple meanings can all become part of your kid's comedic repertoire, so when you ask, "What kind of fish costs a lot of money?" they can tell you with a super cute smile, "A goldfish!"

The fact that many words have more than one meaning is a particularly useful insight that will help bookmonsters as they begin reading. Whenever you see a word (like "sharp"), your brain has to quickly call up all of the associations you have with it (like "pointy," "well-dressed," "smart," and "musically high-pitched") and decipher which meaning best fits the context of what you're reading. Jokes with punchlines that force you to think about multiple meanings of words (like "How do you make a tissue dance? Put a little boogie in it") offer excellent practice for bookmonsters to begin better comprehending what they read. Oh, and if you think a joke about boogers is too gross to include in this book, 'snot.

Bookmonsters Like Riddles, Too

If your kid can't seem to get filled up on jokes, try offering a taste of riddles as well! Riddles and jokes have a lot in common—often requiring you to think creatively and understand clever plays on words. But while jokes are intended to give listeners a quick and easy laugh, riddles challenge them to use logic and problem-solving techniques to try to figure out the answer themselves. Thinking through a riddle's puzzle can sometimes take a while . . . which makes them perfect for helping your kid enjoy brain-boosting benefits, while *you* enjoy some much-needed peace and quiet!

18

Two-Tongued Bookmonsters

S nakes have two-pronged tongues that allow them to locate precisely where smells are coming from. Lemurs use small secondary tongues to help them clean and eat bugs off their primate friends' bodies. And a bookmonster with two tongues has special powers, too. While it shares many of the same language and literacy skills with its single-tongued cousin, it has the added ability to speak more than one language!

Because two-tongued bookmonsters get extra practice with language, they often exhibit enhanced abilities that help them learn how to read, think, and kick serious butt in school and beyond, including:

Metalinguistic skills

No matter how many tongues you have, the phrase *metalinguistic skills* is a mouthful. But it basically means that when you're exposed to the vocabulary and grammar rules of multiple languages, you gain insight into how language works in general. And when you have that under-standing, you can learn more and more languages more and more eas-ily in the future. Ever met someone fluent in seven languages? Meta-linguistic skills made that possible!

Understanding how language works can help children with read-ing as well. After all, learning how to read is a lot like learning a whole new language. Taking on a spoken language requires kids to learn a set of words that symbolize objects in the world, then put them to-gether into sentences to communicate. Learning to read requires kids to memorize a set of letter symbols that represent the sounds they know, then put them together to make meaningful combinations.

Attention and memory abilities

When bilingual kids talk, they have to focus on producing the right set of rules for the language they're speaking, and on mentally suppress-ing the rules of the other language they know. In other words, their brains work really, really hard. Research shows that this extra effort pays off for bilingual people of all ages, as they demonstrate advantag-es in basic cognitive skills like paying attention to relevant informa-tion, following rules, and switching seamlessly between tasks. These skills prove invaluable in areas like school, work, and relationships.

Lifelong brain health

Fortunately, this won't be relevant to your bookmonster for a very, very long time, but it's such a cool perk we had to mention it any-way. Research shows that being bilingual delays the onset of demen-tia and Alzheimer's disease by approximately five years. This makes sense when you consider that elderly people are advised to do cross-word puzzles and other mental games to keep their brains healthy and sharp. Because bilingual people naturally expend more cognitive effort when they communicate, they automatically get additional brain exercise. Now you have a lifetime of reasons to learn a second language!

Start 'em young

If you'd like your bookmonster to enjoy all the benefits that come with speaking multiple languages, here are two words of advice: *Don't wait.* Young children are generally much better than adults at learning a new language. Pick any of the large number of research studies on the subject, and they'll tell you the same thing. No matter what language people are trying to learn, the highest levels of proficiency are achieved when students are exposed to the language early—ideally before the age of eight. If you wait until you're a teenager (when poorly timed American middle and high schools begin requiring kids to take language courses), natural skills and success levels drop off greatly. And after that, good luck, *amigo.* Although a few old fogeys might show impressive natural abilities and learn a new language during their retirement, they are the exception, not the rule.

Part of young children's success at learning a second language can be explained by some incredible innate language-learning processes that operate early in life. At birth, babies are able to hear all of the different sounds from all of the world's languages. In other words, they are poised to learn absolutely any language they encounter. But right around the time their parents help them blow out their first birthday candle, something fascinating happens: Babies start focusing solely on the language they hear every day, and stop being able to distinguish sound differences that aren't relevant to it. It's then that Japanese and

Korean babies stop perceiving the difference between *l* and *r* sounds, because those sounds do not represent a meaningful linguistic difference in their native languages. Believe it or not, there are sounds that speakers of all languages can't hear because the sounds are not relevant to the speaker's language.

Children who are exposed to multiple languages, however, will retain the ability to distinguish all the relevant sound differences for all the languages they hear, making it easier to learn and master them. Research shows that kids don't even have to hear that much of a language to continue recognizing its distinctive sounds. For instance, one study examined what happened when American babies learning English listened to a person reading books and playing with toys while speaking Mandarin Chinese. After hearing the language for a total of just five hours over the course of four weeks, the American babies maintained the ability to distinguish Mandarin sound differences that they would ordinarily lose the ability to hear.

But the fact that young children are in the best possible position to learn a second language still doesn't make it easy. Parents considering raising a two-tongued bookmonster should understand that learning two languages is a much bigger task than learning one, so it will require time, effort, and patience. Because they have to do things like amassing vocabularies and mastering grammatical systems *twice*, it will likely take children who learn multiple languages longer to meet the same language milestones as children learning just one language. And kids who begin to learn a second language after already becoming fluent in a first may experience other slowdowns and difficulties—like suddenly producing errors in their first language as they begin to gain skills in their second.

There are certain circumstances that can help make the process of learning two languages a little easier. In general, children will be more successful when:

More people speak the language

Kids are naturally social, so the more people they hear speaking a language, the more they'll want to speak it, too. Plus, hearing a variety of people speaking the language makes it easier to learn. The acoustic variability of hearing many different examples of the same sounds and words voiced by different people helps second-language learners comprehend and produce these elements themselves.

Kids hear lots of it

The entire "The Perfect Bookmonster Call" chapter (page 18) is devoted to conveying the importance of talking to kids in order to build their language and literacy skills. The same is true for second-language learning. The more a child hears a language, the more quickly they will learn it— and the child must continue to hear this language to retain it.

It is used in high-quality interactions

Studies show that children can learn language well from real-life conversations, but not so much from watching it on a non-responsive television screen. Remember the American babies who kept hearing Mandarin sounds after a speaker read to them and played with toys? The researchers showed another group of babies the *exact same* speaker doing and saying the *exact same* things—except this time, it was on video instead of in person. The babies who watched the video ended up *not* remembering the Mandarin sounds. So make sure your child is exposed to new languages during face-to-face conversations, either in person or via live video chat.

They're motivated to learn it

Some second-language learners are more motivated than others, and it really makes a difference to their success. Generally, learners tend to be more motivated when they're learning a language to interact with others instead of learning it to get a good grade in a class, to gain a parent's approval, or for some other unrelated reason.

Tips for bilingual families

If your family already speaks more than one language, *très bien*! All the talking and reading you do in your home language can make it easier for your kid to learn how to speak and read in a second language. That's because many things remain constant across languages—including the basic understanding of how letters represent language sounds and how distinct sounds can blend together to form new ones. So, stock up on books in your home language and use them often. Every moment you spend talking, laughing, teaching, and building memories in any language will ultimately augment your child's ability to speak and read all the languages they learn.

Tips for monolingual families

Worried that only speaking one language is *no bueno*? Don't fret! Even if you're not a bilingual family, you can still reap some of the same benefits by encouraging your bookmonster to learn a second language. Look for community classes, check out language-learning videos from the library, download a language-learning app, or maybe even enroll your child in a school that specializes in language immersion. Local resources will vary greatly, so check out what your neighborhood has to offer!

Once you've decided on a language to study, it's important to get as much practice for your bookmonster as possible. Seek out family, friends, neighbors, coworkers, parents of friends from school, or anyone you can think of who can converse with your kid. Having casual conversations in the language is the best possible practice, and it also shows kids how exciting it can be to apply the things they've learned to actual interactions with real, live people.

You can also get creative with some second language–inspired adventures! Look around for local places that highlight the language your bookmonster is learning. Go big and save up for a family vacation to somewhere you can be immersed in the language, or simply eat at a restaurant where you can enjoy food from the culture and your child can try ordering in the language. Any of these adventures can work wonders for improving your bookmonster's skills and keeping them motivated. And that is truly *magnifico*!

PART IV

Teaching Your Bookmonster Tricks

After you've given your bookmonster life, a home, and plenty of good stuff to gobble, what's left to do? Have fun, of course! Bookmonsters are experts at learning all sorts of reading-related tricks. And because "learning to read" means the same thing as "having fun" to a bookmonster, they *love* to perform these tricks just as fast as you can teach them. This final collection of chapters will give you a crash course in advanced aspects of reading instruction for kids of all ages. With a little playful practice in the areas we're about to cover, your bookmonster will soon be spelling, writing, punctuating, and dramatizing what they read *in style*!

19

Bookmonsters Love to Spell

Birds blend together whistles, squawks, trills, and honks to produce the delightfully melodic calls and songs we hear each morning. Banded mongooses combine consonant-like grunts with vowel-like screeches to tell other mongooses how the speaker is finding food and avoiding predators. But no creature can truly *spell* the way bookmonsters do. And with the tips you'll find in this chapter, your kiddo can be spelling with the best of them before you know it!

Why it's swell to spell

When adults think about "spelling" these days, they either look backward—remembering their old spelling tests from when they were in school (with fondness or dread, depending on what grades they got)—or they look forward, believing that spell-check and autocorrect features on computers and phones prove that no one needs to know how to spell anything ever again.

But for kids just learning to read, spelling is absolutely relevant. When children learn that individual letters can be put together to spell a word, they also begin to understand how letters can be sounded out to say a word. And in case you need us to *spell it out for you*, that's pretty much exactly what "reading" is. Hop rat! (We meant "Hooray!" Darn you, autocorrect.)

The fact that bookmonsters are able to attempt spelling before they can even read is really cool, super amazing big kid stuff. So tell your kid that! Be sure to talk up your bookmonster's spelling successes by saying how impressed you are with their skills and how awesome it is when they try and try until they figure out a word. Like any other skill, spelling requires effort and practice—and praise from you can be incredibly motivating to your monster!

Just like every other lesson in this book, learning to spell can and should feel like play instead of work. When spelling is framed as an entertaining diversion and not a lame mandatory requirement, it can lead to some staggering reading gains. Here's a list of fun ways to talk about spelling with your bookmonster that don't require any particular location or props, so they can be easily peppered into conversations throughout the day. We started having these kinds of conversations with our kids when they were as young as two or three years old—think about what your own kiddo grasps about letters and letter sounds, and then try these games as soon as you think they're ready:

Words that make you go "hmmm"

Pick a simple word that sounds just like it's spelled, like *on*, *go*, *fun*, *pop*, *yo*, *rad*, or *up*. Then scratch your head, stroke your chin, put on the most quizzical face you can muster, and say, "Hmmm. How do you think you would spell _____?" Seeing you think so hard (and in such a silly, over-the-top fashion) should make your bookmonster eager to join in and help. Coach them through the process as needed by asking them what the first sound is, helping them to isolate subsequent letter sounds, and cheering for every correct letter.

P-O-P quiz

In the middle of running errands, going for a walk, making some art, eating a meal, or just hanging out, turn to your child thoughtfully and say, "Hey. Can you figure out what these letters spell?" Then spell a simple word, like *Y-E-S*, helping your little one to identify each individual sound and blend them all together.

Spelling secrets

Kids might not always want to hear a story about what you did at work, or a lesson they're supposed to learn in school. But they always want to hear a secret! So why not position interesting, quirky info about spelling and language as secrets that you're generously willing to let your kid in on? "Did you realize that *stop* spelled backward is *pots*? Or that *mom* upside down is *wow*?" Wow is right. In our house, we refer to these special spelling coincidences in terms of "secret codes," and we revel in how cool it is when our kids can figure them out!

How spelling leads to reading

After years of talking, playing, and flipping through books together, spelling was the thing that ultimately allowed our kids to put the pieces together to read on their own. For our son, playing spelling games like the ones above were precisely what he needed.

But for our firstborn daughter, the path to solving the reading puzzle was higher tech, yet still centered on spelling. Shortly before our little one's fifth birthday, we started letting her use an app called *Draw Something* to keep connected with cousins who lived in different cities. It's a back-and-forth, Pictionary-style game in which one person draws a picture, and then the other person guesses what it is and draws something else in return. When it's time for you to guess a picture, the app gives you a set of blank spaces corresponding to the number of letters in the correct answer—like four spaces for the word "ring"—plus ten letters to choose from to fill those spaces.

Our secret for turning the app into a great reading lesson was that when our daughter told us her guess for what had been drawn, and then asked us how to spell it, *we did not tell her*. Instead, we asked her how *she* thought the word should be spelled, and then coached her through sounding it out correctly. Over time, our daughter needed less and less support figuring out which letters to push to spell her answers. Eventually she stopped asking us for help altogether—and we'd only know she got the word right because we'd hear the music the app makes when your answer is correct. Around the same time, she started surprising us by successfully reading all kinds of things *outside* the app, too!

Keeping spelling fresh

Once your bookmonster gets big enough to start bringing home real spelling lists from school, some things will change (like the length and complexity of words they're working with), while others will stay the same (like the fact that you should still try to have as much fun with spelling as possible). Instead of simply reading and rereading the list of words your child is supposed to learn, we suggest guiding your bookmonster to study in more entertaining and effective ways. Here are a few ideas that we've used in our house:

Scramble the letters

Try writing the word with the letters rearranged in a mixed-up, random order (like "tobetl" instead of "bottle"), so your kid has to work out the correct spelling to unscramble them.

Find the words in books

On a sheet of paper, have your child write down the name of a book they want to read, along with that week's spelling words underneath it. Each time they find a spelling word in the book's pages, they can add a tally mark next to it on the paper. For added excitement, ask them to gamble their allowance money on which word they think will win. (Obviously, we're kidding. Have them gamble their Halloween candy instead.)

Draw the words

Our eldest bookmonster loves art, so she came up with this one all on her own. Have your mini Monet copy down the entire spelling list, then draw an original artistic interpretation next to each word. Getting so creative will make studying more fun, and the pictures will provide another way to help the words stick in their memories!

Start your own quiz show

Everything's more fun when the whole family gets involved, so show your kid you support their spelling efforts by helping them study. An easy way to do that is by quizzing them on how to spell the words, always remembering to provide corrective feedback and encouragement for incorrect answers and plenty of praise for correct ones. If you want to up the entertainment value, try playing some cheesy game show music when you introduce the "contestants," and describe what "prizes" they can win in your biggest announcer voice. "Congratulations! You've just won a piggyback ride!!!"

Our family enjoys these activities so much that we actually look forward to getting a new spelling list each week. We know, we know, you've never met anyone quite as cool as we are. But as a result, our kids still love spelling—and they're able to keep advancing their reading skills because of it!

Don't Forget the Dictionary!

Even though *you* might not use it much anymore, bookmonsters can definitely benefit from having an old-school, physical dictionary in the house. The next time your child asks you what a word means or how to spell something new, pull out the dictionary, explain how it works, and use it to find the answer. After you get past the onslaught of insults like "Wow, you must be really old to have used this ancient thing when you were a kid" that are sure to follow, your bookmonster might very well start to appreciate the power that comes with being able to find the information they need all on their own.

20

Bookmonsters Love to Write

Beavers build dams to protect themselves from predators and avoid becoming a meal. Spiders weave intricate, insect-snaring webs to catch some food of their own. And termites construct skyscraper-esque mounds of dirt large enough to be seen from space and durable enough to last thousands of years. Bookmonsters are known to make impressive works as well. When you expose them to the imaginative and adventurous world of books early and often, there's nothing they find more fun than creating stories of their own!

Wondering what exactly we mean when we talk about bookmonsters "creating stories"? Perhaps we can best explain it by telling you a story ourselves: Once upon a time, there was a beautiful newborn baby. The baby was soft and squishy on the outside, but had a quickly developing mind that was already sharp as a tack. Whenever the baby's parents talked—to the baby, to each other, to friends, to family members, or to strangers on the street—the baby listened intently.

Much of what the baby heard followed the form of stories. Stories about exciting things they were going to be doing that day, stories about crazy things Mommy and Daddy had done back when they were little kids, stories about irritating things that people in the cars around them were doing right now. So the baby learned what stories sound like. And because the baby's parents read lots and lots of books to the baby, the baby saw what stories looked like, too. Before long, the baby wanted to tell stories just like everybody else—with a voice as soon as the baby learned to speak, and with a big fat permanent marker all over the couch cushions when Mommy and Daddy left the room for they swear only like thirty seconds as soon as the baby learned to write. And so the baby did. And it was wonderful and terrible all at the same time.

Why bookmonsters are good at telling stories

Hearing you tell a story teaches your bookmonster multiple things, including:

- telling stories is a valuable thing to do
- people want to listen to stories
- there are some things you tell stories about (like your trip to the zoo) and some things you don't (like your trip to the potty—unless your poo was a *really* interesting shape)

At about two or three years old, kids begin telling their own simple stories in the form of recalling things that happened to them. Initially, kids' stories tend to lack coherence, leave out important details, and focus only on themselves . . . which is why toddlers would make excellent reality TV show stars. But children gain storytelling skills rapidly, and by about six years old they have already gotten enough experience with stories to know what a good one sounds like, understand the essential elements of stories (like setting, characters, plot building, and problem resolution), and tell a complete story of their own.

Researchers have found that children who are read to more often tend to tell better stories—using more literary language (like "nowhere to be seen"), complex vocabulary ("entrance" instead of "door"), and descriptive details like adjectives ("fierce") and sound effects ("kersplash"). These results are heightened when you read to kids using the techniques in our "The Right Way to Read to a Bookmonster" chapter (page 54). In one particularly compelling study, researchers trained one group of kindergarteners on word and letter sounds, and read to a second group of kindergarteners using the conversational reading strategies we recommend. After sixteen sessions, they tested the children's storytelling abilities by asking them to tell a story about a wordless picture book. The results? Children who experienced interactive reading told stories that were more complex, included more information about characters' feelings and motivations, and incorporated richer vocabulary.

In our family, the effect of all our book reading became adorably apparent when our littlest bookmonster would tell us stories at three years old. Because she'd learned that stories benefit from excitement, she would add multiple suspenseful buildups by leaning in close to us, opening her eyes as wide as they would go, and gasping "*Suddenly . . .*" before giving us the next dramatic detail. Full disclosure: Most of the details weren't all that dramatic—but they sure were cute!

How bookmonsters become even better at telling stories

Improving storytelling skills doesn't have to take a long time. In the research study we just mentioned, the children who showed measurable progress in their storytelling abilities did so after only eight weeks of occasional interactive reading. So imagine the huge positive effect you can have on your child's development by making storytelling a regular part of life! Here are a few more ideas for maximizing your sweetie's story exposure:

Talk about past events

Have plenty of conversations about experiences you and your child have shared. When you do, be sure to cover the information that a complete, elaborate story should. For example, don't just make a laundry list of the structures you played on at the park, because telling someone, "We went down the slide, and rode on the swings, and sat on the teeter-totter" would make a pretty boring story. Instead, give your kiddo experience with more entertaining tales, like those you might tell an adult whose interest you were trying to keep. "We went down the slide together at first because you were too scared to do it on your own, but then you decided to be really brave, and by the end of the day, you were diving down headfirst with your eyes closed, and *I* was the one who was scared!"

Create a story as a group

This game has been a crowd-pleaser for everyone at every age in our family. And it's super simple. One person says the first sentence of a story: "Once there was a chicken nugget named Clark." The next person comes up with the story's second sentence: "Clark's best friend was a surprisingly grumpy milkshake named Swirl." Keep going around the group like that, with each person adding one sentence at a time until you've created a complete story together, somebody ends it, or you're all giggling too hard to continue.

Play pretend

Pretend play involves props, costumes, characters to create, and scenes to invent and act out. So kids get practice with story creation every single time they do it. Check out the "Playtime for Bookmonsters" chapter (page 108) for more benefits and ideas for pumping up your kid's pretend play!

Why bookmonsters should write their stories down

After your kid thinks up some stories, they should practice writing them down with pencil and paper. If you're wondering why we're talking about handwriting in this day and age, when computers allow us to record anything we want by simply typing, texting, or telling our virtual assistant to do it . . . you have a point. Kids will need to start typing stuff up for school assignments before you know it, and computer skills are certainly beneficial. Plus, the computer is a good medium for writing because with practice, typing can become quick and effortless, and it's incredibly easy to revise things you've written on a ~~cornputter~~ computer.

But even with all the benefits of typing, it simply can't replace handwriting. Research studies have compared typing on a keyboard to writing on paper and found some surprising benefits of using regular old paper and pencil. For example, when college students take handwritten notes during a lecture, they perform significantly better on tests compared to students who take notes by typing on a computer. While fast typers may be able to capture nearly every word a professor says, students taking handwritten notes are forced to edit and paraphrase what's being said in the moment—resulting in deeper processing of the material and better-organized notes to study.

Handwriting can have even more benefits for your bookmonster if they learn the art of creating speedy script! Writing is a complex process that requires kids to master both motor skills (performing the appropriate physical movements to correctly draw letters) and language skills (deciding which letters, words, sentences, and paragraphs to write). Children need enough practice to make it quick and automatic, so they can spend less mental energy on the physical act of forming letters and more on planning the content of their writing. Because faster handwriting frees kids up for better thinking and planning, research has found that kids who can write faster outperform slower writers in both test taking and essay writing.

Need one more reason to get motivated to start writing? Research shows that faster writers are less likely than their slower-writing classmates to suffer from low self-esteem. Not too shabby for a few simple pen strokes, eh?

What to expect as your bookmonster learns to write

Writing precise symbols like letters, numbers, and words requires fairly hefty motor skills, plus some understanding of what all those symbols look like to begin with. That's why most little kids attempt to draw pictures first. Even though drawing is not the same as writing, it's important to realize that pictures can still communicate meaning and that drawing has real value to your child's writing future.

For a playful depiction of this concept, check out *Bunny Cakes* by Rosemary Wells. In this book, a young bunny named Max repeatedly goes to the grocery store by himself, with no parental supervision whatsoever (don't ask—just roll with it). He tries to add the "red hot marshmallow shooters" that he's craving to the shopping list he hands the grocer, but because he can't yet write real letters, the grocer doesn't understand. After plenty of trial and error, he finally decides to *draw a picture* of the shooters, and the grocer happily rewards him with what he wants! The idea that pictures can carry powerful meaning is sometimes called "picture power," and it can inspire young kids to believe that the things they draw can be just as important as written words.

Once your kiddo is comfortable drawing pictures, you can gradually introduce elements of writing into the activity. One easy way to do this involves sharing the same piece of paper to draw and write on with your kid. Draw a picture or two, and then add a few letters and words to accompany what you drew—like sketching a speech bubble that says "Tweet" next to a bird, or giving a dinosaur a picket sign that says "Just say NO to asteroids!" Make sure you chat about the cool things you're creating, and emphasize the distinction between writing and drawing: "Our pictures show what things look like, and our writing tells more about them."

At some point, your bookmonster will start trying to write actual letters—which means you'll have to start trying to decode what all those formless swirls, squiggles, and loops are supposed to be. When your child asks you to read something unintelligible that they wrote, you can choose to take a wild guess at what it says, see if you can get them to give you a clue first ("Wow, I wonder what you wrote about!"), or just ask them outright. Whichever tack you go with, just make sure you stay positive about it. Our kids picked up the term "scribble-scrabble" in preschool, using it to describe "little kid" drawings that look more like scribbles than actual pictures. But since it's negative and can make kids self-conscious about their drawing and writing efforts, we avoid the term. Instead, we always compliment any efforts at art or writing our kids make and encourage them to practice, enjoy, and take pride in them—no matter what they look like!

The same thing goes for when kids eventually begin writing letters that resemble the real things. Don't worry if children's early attempts at stringing letters together to make words and sentences aren't correct. The words they write may have some phonetic similarity with what they're trying to spell (like "KT" for "cat") or they may not be close to the real word at all (like "F6Q" for "cat"). Our children's kindergarten teacher referred to this type of invented spelling as "kindergarten perfect," and we love how the term shows it's perfectly OK that new writers spell words any way they like. When you stay supportive, ignore initial inaccuracies, and remember that the important thing is that they're trying, kids can feel free to practice and enjoy writing without becoming overwhelmed by all the spelling and grammar details that will come their way soon enough.

One final thing *not* to worry about: While it's cool to promote good posture and body mechanics while writing, don't get too hung up on little things like precisely how kids hold their pencils. Research shows that the specific pencil grip a child uses is less important than having a comfortable hold that won't lead to cramping or fatigue.

Learning to write can be a difficult and time-consuming skill to master, so it's a good idea to exercise plenty of patience and begin before you feel like you absolutely need to. It's beneficial to start letter-writing practice before milestones like your child starting school or learning how to read, because the act of writing letters can reinforce letter recognition and help prepare kids for reading and school success. Here are some tips for fun and effective handwriting practice at home:

Keep doing everything we've already talked about

Many of the activities mentioned earlier in this book will help your kid work on writing skills, including making writing part of playtime, letting kids write shopping lists, working on activity books, and playing writing games like Tic-Tac-Toe and Hangman.

Copy letters

A basic way to practice forming letters is to have kids copy them from printed text or something you've written. Research shows that copying letters in this way benefits letter recognition more than tracing letters or typing them on a computer.

Stock up on wacky writing supplies

Nothing makes practicing penmanship more fun than outrageous and colorful pens, pencils, erasers, paper, and journals. Keep them in a place that is easy for your child to access without your help, and remember that they also make great gifts for kids!

Make family mailboxes

Our biggest kid inspired this tip by creating "mailboxes" for each family member and hanging them on our bedroom doors. Hers were poster boards folded in half and stapled along the sides, but manila envelopes or folders could work, too. Our kids would surprise us with notes every so often and be absolutely thrilled when they found some from us. After all, who doesn't love getting a sweet letter in the mail?

Make a completely controlled mess

Let your bookmonster practice writing with some ultra-unexpected, super-fun, and usually-very-messy ingredients—in the cleanest way possible! Fill a sealable sandwich baggie with sand, sprinkles, paint, shaving cream, or gelatin mix, and let your bookmonster "write" by pressing down onto the plastic. Or let your child "paint" words all over the place—like on the sidewalk, porch, or side of the house— but substitute water for paint, so the creations can be admired as they're made, before quickly drying up mess-free!

Celebrate your child's success

Show kids you value their writing abilities by encouraging them to make (and then gushing over) homemade birthday and holiday cards, and by proudly displaying kids' writing attempts in your home as you do with their artwork. This can keep kids feeling positive and motivated to continue handwriting practice!

Try Your Hand at Handwriting, Too

Just as it benefits a bookmonster's literacy skills to see you reading, it's good for them to see you writing! An easy way we found to model handwriting on an almost-daily basis is writing lunch notes for our kids. We started out with one in our first child's lunch on her very first day of preschool. Figuring it would be an occasional thing, we did *not* write one the next day. But when she came home complaining about her "missing" lunch note, we got the message—kids really look forward to handwritten parental notes! So now we include one in every lunch, for every kid. If you think you might want to start this tradition, too, please note that it does make lunch prep take longer, especially on days when your exhausted parent brain can't come up with anything interesting to write. But the ways it can help your kid's reading, writing, and relationship with you make it worth it.

The specific kind of notes you write are up to you. Ours are totally random and oftentimes super weird, but we have fun with them and our kids love it. We sometimes include little drawings to go with them, and we write all different kinds of notes, like:

- **Sweet affirmations.** "You're like the frosting to our cupcake. Without you, we'd just be a muffin." & "We love you WAY BIGGER than this note."

- **Corny jokes.** "What's the scariest fruit? A boo-berry!" & "What's the smelliest number? Farty-toot (42)"

- **Random silliness.** "Remember, you're supposed to EAT your food, and WALK on your foot. (Not the other way around!)" & "We'd still love you if you were a tiny little mouse with a giant elephant head. (But we're glad you're not!)"

- **Rhyming poems.** "Spring break is here! You're officially sprung! So let out a cheer, and go have some fun(g)!" & "Here's a tasty spread, to eat with your head. That's what we said! (And that's what you read!)"

- **References to things we've been doing (or reading!)** "For being an awesome builder, excellent student, sweet son and brother, and all-around great kid, you've earned House of Ankowski 1,000 points!" (Inspired by J. K. Rowling's Harry Potter books) & "As you eat this spaghetti, all covered with cheese . . . Hold onto your meatball, and try not to sneeze!" (Inspired by *On Top of Spaghetti* by Paul Brett Johnson)

BONUS TIP: When the lunchboxes come home at the end of the school day, keep the notes! Each of our kids has a freezer bag that gets increasingly full with every lunch note we write. One day we're going to hand them over to our kids, and we hope they think the collection is as sweet a keepsake as we do.

21

Bookmonsters Go Wild for Weird Words

The humpback anglerfish dangles a glow-in-the-dark ball from its nose to lure prey into its fang-filled mouth. The scorpionfly feeds on dead invertebrates while sporting what appears to be a scorpion's stinger (but are actually its genitals). And the platypus is so bizarre—combining a duck's bill, otter's feet, and beaver's tail in a single venomous egg-laying mammal—that the first scientists to study it assumed it must be fake. Just as there are lots of weird-looking animals out there, there are plenty of weird words, rules, and quirks to discover as you learn more and more about language. And bookmonsters can't get enough of them!

What do we mean when we talk about weird words? In this chapter, we're referring to any word that does something out of the ordinary, behaves in an unusual way, or is unfamiliar to you or your bookmonster. This can include things like homonyms, acronyms, figures of speech, words that describe sound effects, and lots more.

When adults come across these constructions while reading books to kids, they sometimes choose to ignore them, assuming that they're too difficult to explain or that they'll just go over children's heads. But weird and wacky word types are sometimes the most interesting part of the book, always help kids understand the story better, and might just make your child even more excited to explore books and stories than they already are! So why not get busy as a buzzing bee, and use them to help communicate the amazingly exciting secret that with language, anything is possible?

Look for these strange word types as you read books with your bookmonster, and be sure to inject them into your increasingly interesting conversations:

New & unusual words

One of the best things that books do for bookmonsters is expand their vocabularies, because books usually use a much wider range of words than people use in everyday speech. *Nanette's Baguette* by Mo Willems is a short picture book that is long on bread, fun sound effects, and interesting words like clarinet, quartet, fret, regret, sweat, reset, and responsibility. Pause the book to explain new vocabulary words, and if *you* don't know what a word means either, or aren't entirely confident in your ability to define it, look it up together! It may be encouraging for kids to realize that even adults don't know all the words, and that they can continue to learn cool stuff no matter how smart (or staggeringly old) they get.

Synonyms

Knowing multiple words that mean the same thing is excellent (and fantastic, awesome, spectacular, and wonderful) for becoming a good storyteller and writer. Synonyms are also a useful tool for explaining new words to your kid while you read! Check out *Thesaurus Rex* by Laya Steinberg—as the name implies, it features a dinosaur who knows a pretty impressive repertoire of synonyms.

Antonyms

There are entire books devoted to teaching kids about opposites. When our bookmonsters were little, they couldn't get enough of the cute gender-unspecified baby in Leslie Patricelli's board books that feature antonym pairs, like *Big Little*, *Yummy Yucky*, and *No No Yes Yes*. But keep in mind that antonyms can be an integral part of your book-related conversations even after your kid has graduated beyond board books!

Homonyms

The English language has a huge number of words that sound the same but mean two different things (called homophones), or that sound different even though they're spelled the same (also known as homographs). The cute Halloween book *Which Way to Witch School?* by Scott Santoro features one such word pair right in the title. And if you've ever taken a *bow* after tying your shoelaces in a *bow*, you've demonstrated another. Point these out for kids and show them how spelling and context can help them figure out which word is ~~witch~~ which.

Similes & metaphors

Even children's books draw comparisons between two seemingly different things to make descriptions more vivid or to help explain complex topics. Similes do this using the words *like* or *as*, while metaphors create a connection without those words. You can help kids better understand stories that feature analogies like these by guiding them toward what the author means. For example, when a boy helps a stray cat and her newborn kittens escape a thunderstorm in *One Dark Night* by Hazel Hutchins, you can ask your kid to imagine what each kitten is like based on their striking similes—"soft as whispers, gray as dawn," "soft as stuffing, white as snow," and "wet as water, black as night." And when the title character in Jane Manning's *Millie Fierce* looks sadly at a walked-all-over smudge on the sidewalk and says "That's me," you can sigh about how she's feeling melancholy over a metaphor.

Idioms

Common phrases that use figurative language to communicate something very different from their words' literal definitions are so familiar to us adults that we sometimes forget how crazy they must sound to kids. For example, when you read *The Berenstain Bears' Report Card Trouble* by Stan and Jan Berenstain, your kid will be shocked to discover that when "Brother was in the soup, deep in the soup up to his eyeballs," it had absolutely nothing to do with food, or eyes!

Palindromes

Ever notice that some things like "dad," "racecar," "taco cat," and "yo banana boy" are spelled the same both forward and backward? Well, chances are your bookmonster hasn't noticed this yet . . . but once you point it out, they'll be as excited as an "oozy rat in a sanitary zoo!" In addition to fun individual phrases to laugh about with your kid, you can also look for palindromes in poems and songs. Although it starts with a brief bit of PG-13 language that parents might want to cough

loudly over, the song "I Palindrome I" by They Might Be Giants cel-
ebrates some seriously inventive palindromes like "egad a base tone
denotes a bad age," and an entire verse where the letters aren't the
same in reverse but the words are: "'Son I am able,' she said, 'though
you scare me.' 'Watch,' said I. 'Beloved,' I said, 'watch me scare you
though.' Said she, 'able am I, son.'"

Anagrams

When our son realized that letters making up one word or phrase
could be mixed up to create a totally different word or phrase, *he was
all in* (anagram: *alien shawl*). He started creating them himself, and
we started writing his all-time favorite lunch notes with increasingly *bizarre combinations* (anagram: *bob romanticizes rain*). To get your
little one hooked on anagrams too, check out *Ann and Nan Are Anagrams: A Mixed-Up Word Dilemma* by Mark Shulman.

Abbreviations

Kids won't know that spellings like Dr., Mr., info, and Feb. are short
for other words until you tell them. It's easy to miss a fun part of the
title of *Judy Moody, M.D.: The Doctor Is In!* by Megan McDonald if you
don't know how the words *medical doctor* can be abbreviated. Good
thing explaining it to your bookmonster only takes a sec!

Onomatopoeia

This crazy-sounding word is used for words that sound like the thing
they describe. *Boing, yawn, zap, jingle, thwack, burp,* and many, many
others fit the bill. If you want a whole bunch of onomatopoeia all
in one book, check out the moos, croaks, honks, and beeps of Alice
Schertle's *Little Blue Truck.*

Acronyms

Acronyms might just be the wackiest word category that you'll encounter while reading, because they're made up of the initials of a whole other set of words that aren't always even present. BTW, let kids in on these ASAP or IDK how much they'll understand. Dav Pilkey's books use acronyms in some fantastically silly ways—like when one character invents the PATSY (Photo-Atomic Trans-Somgobulating Yectofantriplutoniczanziptomiser) 2000 to turn 2D pictures into living 3D objects in *Captain Underpants and the Attack of the Talking Toilets.*

Why kids get so wild with language

Which of the following best sums up how you feel about children learning to love reading?

"Neat!"
"Groovy!"
"Outtasight!"
"Rad!"
"Sick!"
"On fleek!"

There's a good chance the answer you chose has a lot to do with how old you are. Whatever words you used to mean "cool" when you were young are probably the same ones you think are cool now. New slang terms like these pop up constantly in our culture. And kids are largely the ones coming up with them. Slang is an everyday example of how young people demonstrate their natural drive to create language—with every generation inventing completely new vernaculars of their own.

Because kids are naturally innovative with language, they've been instrumental to the creation of many languages throughout history. Although most of the world's languages have been around so long that it isn't possible to track their origins, one group of researchers had the incredible opportunity to observe an entirely new language being born. And kids had everything to do with it.

In the late 1970s, Nicaragua opened their first public school for the deaf. The deaf students at the school had hearing parents, and the teachers at the school taught primarily through lipreading. But the students were allowed to communicate through hand gestures during informal situations like riding on the bus and eating lunch, which soon led to the kids forming a set of signs to symbolize common words. It was a very basic system of communication, but it enabled them to begin understanding and interacting with one another.

When the next cohort of students arrived, something remarkable happened. The young students quickly learned the established signs so they could communicate with their peers, but they didn't stop there. As they used the language, they naturally added grammatical complexity to convey additional information. For example, signers who wanted to describe a "fast car" could produce the gesture for "car" using the space slightly to their left followed by the gesture for "fast" in the same location to indicate that the two words belong together. This type of action is a crucial component of fully developed sign languages, in which signers intentionally use precise places in space to express meaning. So the new speakers didn't just use the language, they also improved it! And with the additional grammatical structure, the students' gestural communication was transformed into the true, complex language that today is known as Nicaraguan Sign Language.

Are you assuming that deaf signers in Nicaragua are just one isolated example of the only kids who ever managed to create a language? Picture us signing this: Cut. It. Out. There have been several times in history when people who shared no common language had to come together to communicate—and kids played a crucial role in combining the group's separate languages into something everyone could use, every single time.

Sometimes kids devise whole new ways of speaking that are not full languages but still sufficient to disguise whatever they're saying from adults. Take Pig Latin, for instance. That's where you talk in English sentences but systematically mix everything up by moving the first sound in each word to the end and then adding "ay" to it. For example, "Bookmonsters love reading!" becomes, "Ookmonstersbay ovelay eadingray." When Amber was a kid, she and her friends came up with their own Pig Latin-y way of speaking by inserting "dig" in the middle of every syllable, as in "Boodigookmodigonstedigers lodigove readigeadidiging!" Although it sounds incredibly silly as an adult, at the time it had the desired effect of totally tricking Amber's parents. But we guess turnabout is fair play, because like so many generations of children before them around the world, our own kids made up their own language. They'd spend whole playdates with friends working on it and taunting us with what sounded like nonsense words that we never fully deciphered. Although we did figure out that when we heard "blurgee blurgee," it meant the kids wanted ice cream. (Didn't we all?)

If you want to encourage your kid's creativity with language, but still be able to understand what the heck they're saying, try some of these otallytay unfay ordway amesgay:

Tongue twisters

Getting all tripped up on tongue twisters with friends and family is more fun than picking a peck of pickled peppers, or selling seashells by the seashore. Those classic tongue twisters are obviously good ones to start sharing with your kid, but there are plenty more out there to explore. *Oh Say Can You Say?* by Dr. Seuss contains a wide variety of tongue twisters ready-made for you and your bookmonster to challenge each other. You can also create your own tongue twisters by thinking of phrases full of similar-sounding words. Our kids thought up things like "seven silly sweaty socks," "five farts felt fine," and "action, adventure, and some apples." We all take turns seeing how many times we can say each phrase before getting scrambled up. Just remind your kid that it's only for fun, so you can delight in everybody's mistakes—including your own!

Silly segmentation

A major task of learning a language is figuring out where words begin and end, or how to segment a whole sentence into its individual words. Our son invented this language game when he realized that some words could be segmented in different places to drastically alter their meanings. Get creative with your bookmonster to figure out your own unexpected combinations, such as:

- "Nowhere is *now* and *here*."
- "To welcome is *towel come*."
- "Carpet is *car* and *pet*."
- "Mountain is *mount a in*."

Spoonerisms

If you've ever accidentally mixed up parts of two words you were trying to say, like "I need to nake a tap," then you already have experience with spoonerisms (and yes, you probably do need to take a nap, too). For bookmonsters, coming up with these jumbled, jokey phrases *on purpose* can be foads of lun—we mean, loads of fun. And if you need a little inspiration first, be sure to flip through *Smart Feller Fart Smeller* by Jon Agee!

Word jar

Sometimes families keep a "word jar" of words that are particularly interesting, complex, or have dual meanings. Using scraps of paper, write down examples of the weird word types from this chapter as they appear in books or pop into your mind, and put them in the jar. Then pull out a new word each day to discuss with your kiddo. If you want, you can make it a friendly competition to see who can work the wild word into conversations the most times, or in the most interesting ways, all day long. Be sure to celebrate—by cheering, screaming, dancing, or giving high fives—every time somebody says the word!

22

Bookmonsters Keep It Real

R accoons can learn to pick complex locks in fewer than ten attempts. Pigs as young as six weeks old can learn to use mirrors to help them get through a maze. And crows can learn to memorize the routes of garbage trucks for miles throughout a city. Why do they do it? Well, in the case of all these animals, the answer is *food*. But bookmonsters like to learn about real-life stuff, too, and their motivations for doing so are something else entirely.

The desire to know things is ingrained in us from birth. From the moment we enter the world, we start trying to learn things like *Whose voices do I recognize in this room? Where did my comfy womb go? What happens if I put this nipple in my mouth?* (Oh yeah . . . bookmonsters are motivated by food, too.) And the search for knowledge doesn't stop there. As kids get older, they demonstrate their lust for learning by asking parents what sometimes feels like a nonstop barrage of questions.

On a basic level, knowing things like how to get something to eat, stay warm at night, and avoid being trampled by a hippopotamus is key to our survival. On a more advanced level, we seek to gain understanding about the best ways to build relationships with other people, find love, achieve occupational and financial success, and be happy. When you look at it this way, learning is what life is all about. And when bookmonsters are in the mood to learn something, nonfiction books are the first place they look.

Saying "yes" to nonfiction

Nonfiction books are all about communicating facts. Which may make some of you wonder, "Why do we even need to teach children factual information anymore? Can't they just learn to look up whatever they need to know on the internet?" While it's true that technology makes accessing info quicker and easier than ever, there are several reasons why having a healthy store of knowledge inside your boring old brain can still be beneficial. For example, knowing facts can help with:

Comprehension

The more things you know, the easier it is to understand new things you encounter. In our chapter on "The Perfect Bookmonster Call" (page 18), we explained how having a large vocabulary benefits reading because children can better recognize familiar words when they see them in text. The same basic idea applies to facts. When children understand more about the world and how it works, they are able to understand more about the stories and ideas they read.

Learning new things

Having a wealth of knowledge is beneficial for incorporating new information. For instance, it would be easier to understand and remember what a particular woodworking tool is for if you already have a good basic command of carpentry. No matter what specific topic you're learning about, it's helpful if you already have some knowledge to draw from.

Critical thinking

We all hope that our kids develop into savvy critical thinkers instead of malleable sheep passively agreeing with whatever they read and hear. It's more likely that children will be able to do so if they gain experience learning and discussing factual information.

Problem solving

In school and in life, children will be faced with many different kinds of difficulties. That's why it's important that they become adept at identifying problems, generating solutions, and creating effective resolutions. Although general skills like creativity and perseverance are important for solving all kinds of problems, having content knowledge and the ability to acquire more of it are often just as valuable.

As if all those benefits aren't enough, here's another one that should hit close to home(room): Experience with reading and discussing nonfiction books on topics your bookmonster is interested in now can pay off with higher grades later. Kids will eventually need to learn lots of information from textbooks and sift through reference materials to compose research papers, so getting children used to learning and reading about facts is a great way to prep for school.

It's important to have nonfiction books in your home library and use them when you read out loud to your kid. The fact that children typically get far more exposure to fictional stories than to nonfiction texts is particularly true for girls, because factual books are often gender-stereotyped as "boy" books. But given the educational benefits of experience with reading factual works, striking a balance between fiction and nonfiction books is crucial for bookmonsters of any gender. Parents can even pair fiction and nonfiction books in a way that enhances them both. For example, after you read the fictional story *The Very Hungry Caterpillar* by Eric Carle, you could read the factual book *My, Oh My—A Butterfly!: All About Butterflies* by Tish Rabe. Doing so will not only help kids learn more about the real life cycle of caterpillars becoming butterflies, it will also teach them a much more valuable lesson . . . that reading nonfiction books can be both educational *and* fun!

To give children accessible tastes of science, history, and other factual subjects, look for entertaining expository books geared toward younger readers. For example, the Who Was? series published by Grosset & Dunlap contains biographies of prominent historical figures that can help kids see history as a collection of interesting stories and not just boring dates to memorize. Books like *The Curious Kid's Science Book: 100+ Creative Hands-on Activities for Ages 4–8* by Asia Citro use interactive experiments to show children how useful, exciting, and tactile science can be.

Contemporary nonfiction books for children go well beyond the bounds of the classroom to cover lots of other information kids might be curious about. With such a huge variety of subjects to pique your child's interest, learning new facts can be surprisingly entertaining and enlightening for both kids and parents alike. Our family has especially enjoyed exploring the following topics:

Construction

Over time, our crazy kids have been drawn to numerous books about construction, including everything from fictional stories like *Goodnight, Goodnight, Construction Site* by Sherri Duskey Rinker to actual full-blown instruction manuals on home remodeling and pest control. But their favorite kind of construction books are ones about LEGO building. There are dozens of instructional books that show kids how to make innumerable creations using the LEGO bricks they likely already own. One of our kids' favorites is *The LEGO Ideas Book: Unlock Your Imagination* by Daniel Lipkowitz.

Cooking

Our two oldest bookmonsters have both gotten way into cooking. Our daughter enjoys making recipes for filled cupcakes, tarts, and other impressive confections that she reads about in cookbooks like *Kid Chef Bakes: The Kids Cookbook for Aspiring Bakers* by Lisa Huff. Our son, on the other hand, loves seeking out the strangest cookbooks he can find. *The Gross Cookbook* by Susanna Tee motivated him to throw an entire gross-themed party—he cooked a multiple-course meal for his friends and filled a nose-shaped piñata with green candy. You never know what your own kid might be inspired to create!

Crafts

To say that our kids are super into arts and crafts is an understatement. They've read books on sewing, painting, origami, making creations from cardboard, and lots more. Basically, if you can make a giant mess of the house with it, they're all in. *The Toilet Roll Activity Book: Over 30 Wonderful Things to Create* by Lauren Farnsworth and

Crafting with Cat Hair: Cute Handicrafts to Make with Your Cat by Kaori Tsutaya both illustrate how you can make surprisingly inventive crafts with even the most mundane household items.

This list doesn't even begin to cover all the topics kids can explore through nonfiction. We challenge you to head to your local library and take a gander around the children's nonfiction section. You will surely be amazed by the truly *huge* selection available to kids these days, and you will also hopefully find some things that speak to your bookmonster's unique interests!

Finding facts beyond books

Remember that books aren't the only way to learn. Raising a bookmonster is a way of life that includes enjoying words, language, and ideas wherever they can be found—and factual information can be found almost anywhere. To inspire you to get out there and look for it, here are some ideas for places other than a bookshelf where you and your knowledge-loving little one can interact with informational talk and text:

Museums

There are so many interesting kinds of museums to explore, including art, science, history, and culture—and *all* of them include print-rich exhibits!

Zoos, aquariums, and wildlife refuges

Bookmonsters learn as much from talking and laughing as they do from sitting and reading, so enjoy the wildlife together and discuss what you see.

Hiking trails

Going out and exploring nature is a great way to bring science facts to life. Nature can teach kids many lessons—especially if there are posted placards along the way!

Historical landmarks

Help kids understand the relevance of history by demonstrating that it's all around us. Explore local historical landmarks and make a point to see some when visiting new places.

Documentaries

Choosing nonfiction content, like documentary movies and shows, is an excellent way to make the most of screen time. Our family really flipped over the BBC documentary *Dolphins: Spy in the Pod*, which featured a bunch of "spy creatures" the filmmakers built to look like common ocean creatures—but were actually video cameras secretly recording never-before-seen wild dolphin activity.

Classes

Every new activity comes with its own jargon to learn and expertise to acquire. You can find classes for kids on virtually any topic, including sports and exercise, arts and crafts, theater, technology, cooking, chess, and so much more. Plus, getting kids involved in activities can be a great way to keep their minds and bodies healthy and active.

Travel

Nonfiction is all about the real world around us, and the best way to learn about it is to go live in it. So get out there and never stop seeing new things, talking to new people, and experiencing facts firsthand!

23

Bookmonsters Sweat the Small Stuff

Fairyflies are less than one millimeter long, yet their appetite for other insects' eggs makes them a valuable form of pest control for farmers. Golden poison frogs may be small enough to fit on a dime, but they contain enough poison to kill at least ten full-grown men. And little baby hedgehogs are really, really cute.

Seriously. Look 'em up. You'll see.

If you ignore these tiny creatures, you'll miss out on things that could help you, hurt you, or make you say, "Awwwwwww. Who's a pwetty wittle hedgehog?" Likewise, if bookmonsters ignore tiny details in written language, they'll miss out on some extremely important stuff. That's why you'll want to be sure to discuss the finer points of punctuation, grammar, pictures, and more as you continue to read with your child. Because you've been showing that reading can be an interactive, conversational experience, kids will be happy to stop every so often to really revel in the book's details.

Don't think about these topics as a onetime-only conversation. You'll encounter these details over and over again as you read different books, so you should bring them up whenever they catch your attention or seem like they might add interesting information to the particular story you're sharing. As they appear repeatedly over time, you'll find that your child will gain comprehension, and you'll naturally want to talk about them in more sophisticated ways.

In the illustrations

Illustrators are purposeful about a book's pictures, and the details they choose to include go a long way toward reinforcing and complementing the words of a story. Some of our favorite illustration-related topics to discuss are:

Lines

It's amazing how much a well-placed line can communicate.

Curved lines can suggest movement, bouncing lines can trace the trajectory that a moving object has taken to get to its location, and a puffy cloud shape at the end of a line can tell you that someone or something just moved superfast. Lines pointing outward from a character's face can indicate surprise, a mass of dark scratchy lines over a character's head can show anger, and squiggly lines coming off a character's body can let you know that somebody needs a shower!

Characters

Look closely at characters' facial expressions, body language, and any extra details that may be included in the illustrations. Help kids practice empathy by discussing what clues the illustrations provide about characters' thoughts, feelings, and motivations. "Does this character look happy or sad? Why do you think the character feels that way?"

Speech & thought bubbles

If you're looking for insight into characters' feelings and motivations, there's nothing more informative than bubbles that show exactly what they're saying and thinking! Always read what's inside these bubbles out loud so that non-reading kids can know what they say, and be sure to point to the words as you read them to visually connect which character the words are coming from. Discuss how you can tell whether a character is speaking the words (because the bubble includes an arrow pointing to the speaker's mouth), or just thinking them (because there are little circles between the bubble and the thinker's head).

Our son got lots of practice with thought bubbles versus talking bubbles during his long obsession with Garfield comic books. In the comics, Garfield the pet cat can't talk, so while his human owner Jon always uses speech bubbles, Garfield always uses thought bubbles. We loved to vary our reading by imagining what each comic strip must be like from Jon's perspective—because we knew Jon couldn't hear what his cat was thinking, we would cover up Garfield's bubbles with our fingers. Sometimes this made us crack up more than the cartoon itself, other times we'd realize that Jon's reaction didn't make a whole lot of sense if he really couldn't hear Garfield, and once in a while we even spotted inconsistencies showing Garfield accidentally pictured *talking with a speech bubble*! It was really fun to see how tuned into the specifics of each bubble our little bookmonster became because he knew they were essential to understanding the jokes.

Connections to the text

Just like the words in a book, the pictures tell a rich story of their own—and it can be fun to evaluate how well the two match. Take a good look at the pictures and talk about what information you can learn from them that isn't in the text, or what details you hear in the words that are left out of the pictures. As bookmonsters get bigger and start reading books with fewer and fewer illustrations, they'll start building more of the story in their minds, so it can be cool to ask them how they're picturing things in there. "How does this illustration compare to what you were imagining the scene would look like? What's the same? What's different?" You can even try drawing pictures yourselves, either in the same style the illustrator has made them or however else you might like to see them!

In the text

As you talk about text with your bookmonster, you may be surprised how often it makes sense to bring up minute textual details, because they're often crucial to fully understanding the story. Although paying attention to punctuation and grammar might sound too advanced for a preschool-aged pre-reader, parents can start discussing them with kids of any age by using basic, conversational language. Just point out the concept, tell your kid what it means, give additional examples, and most important, be playful! Here are some of the details worth discovering:

Exclamation points

These are seemingly small details that even little monsters can appreciate. Imagine you were reading *Peanut Butter & Cupcake!* by Terry Border. You could point to the exclamation point in the title and explain it using simple language like, "See this line with a dot underneath? That's called an exclamation point, and it means that you should say the words before it like you're really excited. Because there's an exclamation point after the words *Peanut Butter & Cupcake* right here, how do you think we should say them?" Then give your kid license to have a blast saying the words as excitedly (which will most likely mean *loudly*) as possible. After this experience, kids will be thrilled to see the same exclamation point on subsequent readings of the same book, and they may even remember to say the title excitedly with little or no prompting. You can also begin talking about exclamation points you find in other books by asking kids what they mean and comparing them to other punctuation like question marks and periods.

Question marks

Put a great big curve in your exclamation point line, and now you've got a question mark on your hands. Tell your kid that when you see one of these at the end of a sentence, it means you're supposed to say the words like they're a question. Then have fun practicing a bit, inflecting up on your sentences' last words and maybe even raising your eyebrows and shrugging your shoulders to really get your point across. If you happen to come across a Spanish sentence that's a question, you can talk about how it has not only a regular question mark at the end, but also an upside-down question mark at the beginning. ¿How amazing is that?

Periods & commas

The single dot used to end most sentences and its bent, break-inducing cousin may not be nearly as dramatic as their exclamation point and question mark friends, but bookmonsters are still happy to learn about them. "Check it out. This period means it's the end of the sentence, so you can pause for a second and take a breath. *Sigh!*"

Other punctuation

There are many other types of punctuation to discuss besides the basic ones above. We know that just hearing the word "punctuation" makes some people want to fall asleep, but if you connect it to the story and talk about it in a conversational way, we promise it doesn't have to be boring.

> Apostrophes are used primarily to show possession (this is Daddy's favorite chair), or that letters have been left out of a contraction (Daddy's sleeping in his favorite chair).

" " Quotation marks come in pairs, and tell you that everything between them is the exact wording somebody said, as in "Whoa!" exclaimed the wide-eyed surfer dude.

( ) Parentheses also appear in pairs, showing that whatever's between them is an aside, afterthought, joke, or additional idea (kind of like these words right here).

• Colons are used right before a list or explanation of something. People also used to combine a colon with a single parenthesis to make a sideways smiley face, back before they invented way cooler-looking emojis. :)

• Semicolons are kind of like a cross between a comma and a period. They tend to be used in more formal pieces of writing; therefore, you won't find them in kids' books very often. Also, they can make your sideways smiley faces wink at you. ;)

Capitalization

There are many aspects of capitalization to discuss with bookmonsters, like the fact that sentences, names, and titles all start with capital letters. But things get extra interesting when you talk about how capital letters are used to show emphasis—like to indicate that text is PARTICULARLY important, or that a character is YELLING REALLY LOUDLY! Then kids can really get into the conversation, since it means that they get to yell again!

Spaces

It might seem strange to spend time thinking about something as simple as the blank spaces between words. But bookmonsters need to know that those spaces have an important job to do—separating words so they don't all run together. This might be particularly tough for kiddos to remember when they first begin writing words on their own, so a good trick is to have new writers lay a pointer finger on the paper after each word they write, giving them a nice space before starting the next one.

Prefixes and suffixes

Groups of letters that are commonly added to the beginnings (prefixes) or endings (suffixes) of words are especially interesting to bookmonsters, since they change the meaning of the words they're attached to in consistent and predictable ways. As kids advance through school, they'll be expected to read textbooks and learn multiple new words every day. This process is much easier if they're already familiar with common word parts that will allow them to more quickly decipher the meanings of new words. For example, if you learn that the word "integrate" means to combine things together, and you already know that the prefix "dis-" means "not," then you can figure out that "disintegrate" means to break something apart. Here are some other prefixes and suffixes you may want to casually converse about:

a-	-ed	im-	post-
-able/-ible	-er/est	-ish	pre-
anti-	-er/or	-ist	re-
co-	extra-	-less	-s/-es
con-	-ful	-ly	-tion
de-	in-	mis-	un-
dis-	-ing	non-	

Symbols

There are many symbols you'll find in print that kids probably won't be familiar with. Even if you can't remember every symbol's technical name, or never did figure out the right way to pronounce "ampersand," you can still talk about what they mean:

& The ampersand is a crazy curly way to simply say "and."

@ The "at" sign can be used in email addresses and social media handles, and comes in handy when kids want to do some quick accounting work on their lemonade stand invoices.

This little beauty has all sorts of uses, including indicating numbers, social media hashtags, sharp notes in music, and even how many pounds something weighs!

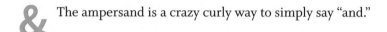 Dollars and cents signs are all about that money. Your kid will surely bring them up all the time after learning what an allowance is.

% The percent sign tells you how much out of 100 something is (as in, "These kids are 99% on my nerves today. Good thing they're 100% adorable.")

✱ Asterisks placed after a word or sentence usually mean "look down"—because there's more to the story next to *another* asterisk someplace else. Like this fine print at the bottom of whatever toy box your kiddo just opened: *27 "D" batteries not included.*

/ The slash can be used in many ways, including meaning "or" or "and," representing fractions in math, separating days/months/years in dates, indicating line breaks in song lyrics and poetry, forming addresses of websites, and playing lead guitar in rock bands with singers named Axl.

— Dashes can be used to indicate an intended pause or break in thought, much like colons or parentheses do— and if you haven't noticed already, we love 'em!

• • • Ellipses are amazing for . . . dramatic pauses!

&@#$%* Put a whole bunch of symbols together, and you've got the perfect speech bubble content for a character who just stubbed a toe!

On the book itself

Normally when kids ask you to read them a book, they mean from "Once upon a time" through "happily ever after." But there are loads of other letters and numbers printed on those pages that you *could* read, if you really wanted to. And because bookmonsters love learning anything and everything they can about reading, at some point they're going to want you to read some of this stuff, too:

Author & illustrator names

Reading the names of the people who worked so hard to entertain you is not only a nice little shout-out to them but also an alert to your child that creating books is an actual job they could do someday!

Page numbers

Show your kid's math and counting skills a little love by pointing out the page numbers in the corners. They're also useful for remembering your place in longer books when you don't have a bookmark handy.

Tables of contents

In chapter books, or books that are collections of short stories, these page locations listed before the main book starts are perfect for jumping straight to the section you're looking for.

Indexes

Usually found in nonfiction and technical texts, these lists located at the end of the book show the page numbers where all sorts of topics and ideas appear in alphabetical order.

Copyright info

Admittedly, most people will hardly ever choose to read this deepest cut of the book detail catalogue. But if you look behind your book's title page, you and your bookmonster can find out when and where it was published as well as who the publisher is, plus read some riveting prose about how you are not allowed to copy any of it, in any manner whatsoever. We've actually flipped over to this page in a handful of children's books ourselves, mostly when they contained either charmingly old-timey phrases or horribly antiquated gender stereotypes—and we wanted to know when the heck somebody wrote this thing!

24

Bookmonsters Say It Like They Mean It

Eagles soar majestically to awe-inspiring heights. Gazelles leap so gracefully that people write love poems about them. And whales shoot shimmering, stories-tall fountains into the air every time they take a breath. When animals are at their confident, comfortable best, they are truly beautiful to watch.

The same thing is true about bookmonsters.

The first time you watch your child read *real words* right off the page, it's an undeniably thrilling feeling. But bookmonsters never stop there. A lasting love of reading can only come after children develop a deep understanding of the meaning all those words represent. When absorbing written language becomes as natural and effortless to them as breathing. And when they truly feel the text flowing through their minds and hearts, page after page after page.

Years after kids read their first words, they will still be building skills in more advanced aspects of literacy, including reading text fluently, answering questions about content, and empathizing with characters to dramatize the things they've read. And you can help them achieve all of this. Although adults sometimes think they're completely out of the reading picture once children are able to do it on their own, the truth is that kids will still benefit from support and shared reading experiences well beyond their early days of reading words independently. So there's your official, scientifically backed reason to accumulate as many more joyous reading experiences together with your kid as possible. (You're welcome!)

Reading fluently

Learning to read easily, smoothly, and accurately is an important step to becoming a skilled reader. This natural-sounding style of reading is not just pleasing to the ear—it's also vital for enabling kids to comprehend what they read. Because fluent readers don't have to expend their mental energy on sounding out words, they can concentrate more fully on text meaning and absorb a lot more of the actual content.

When children can read fluently, they have gained the ability to recognize words, understand their meanings, feel associated emotions, and realize how they connect to the rest of the text. That's a lot to do all at once. So it's no wonder that becoming a fluent reader requires a tremendous amount of practice—both reading independently and with others. Here are some tips for helping your bookmonster become fantastically fluent:

Show them how it's done

As a fully grown, literate adult, you're an ideal model of what a good, fluent reader sounds like. So keep reading together often, since the more your kid hears proper pacing, pronunciation, and inflection, the more they will internalize those things and incorporate them into their own reading. Modeling can also be an effective tool when kids are struggling with a particular passage. You can read the sentence aloud first and have them read it right after, or you can try reading in unison to help your young reader get the right rhythm.

Just add audiobooks

Listening to audiobooks can provide your bookmonster with another example of fluent reading (while also giving you a chance to rest your voice). Make this activity even more valuable by having kids follow along with a physical copy of the book at the same time. Some libraries offer audiobook/picture book pairings to check out together precisely for this purpose—ask your librarian!

Familiarity is your friend

When you're focusing on improving fluency, it can be helpful to use short, familiar passages that your child knows—like songs or nursery rhymes. Since kids already have a good idea what the written words say, they can concentrate more on *how* they're saying them, getting useful practice delivering the words as fluently as possible.

Gather an audience

The more kids read aloud, the more confident they'll become in their abilities. So give your little lecturer plenty of practice with all sorts of reading partners—you, grandparents, siblings, babysitters, friends, pets, stuffed animals, or even fields of corn. (They're all ears, after all.)

It's completely normal for kids to make lots of mistakes on their way to becoming fluent readers, and these mistakes will naturally resolve themselves as kids get more practice reading. Common errors can include skipping words, inserting extra words, incorrectly identifying or sounding out words, and substituting words with ones that resemble the correct one in meaning (like substituting "mommy" for "mother") or letter arrangement (like saying "horse" instead of "house"). These errors may be more common if kids are trying to go too quickly. If you think that might be the case, gently remind your speed reader to relax and slow down. Remember, the goal is to have a good time and discover an amazing story—not race as fast as we can to the end.

If you want to correct a reading error, be casual about it so you don't make your kid feel like they've done anything wrong, as in, "Oh yeah, that word does look like 'homey,' but sometimes when there's an *e* at the end of a word, you don't say it. They call it a *silent e*, and 'home' has one. Isn't that interesting?" Timing is also important, so try not to blurt out "You made a mistake!" as soon as you hear it. Instead, wait until the end of the clause or sentence, and see if your bookmonster notices the error first. If not, go ahead and offer your advice in a positive and supportive way. Depending on the error, you can suggest that your child look at the word more closely, sound it out, use the context of the sentence or story to figure out what it might be, provide other information that you think could be helpful, or simply explain what the word is.

When our kids were new readers, we found that they often got hung up on words like "singing" and "hopped" that seemed deceptively long and daunting, but were actually made up of words and word parts they already knew. In cases like that we would cover up the ending with our fingers and say, "Try reading it now." After they realized that the beginning said "sing" or "hop," we would then talk about how to pronounce the ending, before finally encouraging them to put the whole word together. With common endings, we would also remind them of things like, "Because *i n g* always says *ing*, you can just try to memorize that sound, so when you notice another word that includes it, it will be easier to read!"

Comprehending what you read

Just because kids can read rapidly and fluidly doesn't mean they're understanding and remembering everything. Comprehension is a separate skill from fluency, and it's absolutely necessary for kids' enjoyment of the things they read now, and for success in school later on. Students have to be able to consciously monitor their own thinking and learning as they read and study—constantly comparing what they're trying to learn with what they already know, and filling in gaps accordingly. Even when reading a storybook for fun, bookmonsters need to be able to evaluate their understanding of a text sentence by sentence, tracking the entire story as it unfolds and assessing whether they are missing any important bits of info. Since this paragraph was particularly full of complex information, now's the perfect time for *you* to monitor your own comprehension—if you think you may not have understood everything you just read, go back and read it again!

Although parents may assume that some kids are naturally better at these kinds of skills and that's the end of the story, the truth is that reading comprehension is a skill that any child can be taught. They just need instruction! Research shows that there are cross-cultural differences in the amount of explicit instruction that kids get in things like monitoring their own thinking, study skills, and problem-solving strategies. Specifically, German parents tend to provide children with more of this sort of information, and their children benefit as a result. (They also provide them with lots of delicious sausages, so that's another bonus.) If you personally didn't get much instruction like this when you were a kid, then you may have figured out how to manage reading and studying on your own along the way. But wouldn't it have been faster and easier if someone had just talked to you about how to do it? Here are some simple ways you can coach your own kid to think about and improve comprehension while reading:

Take a mental picture . . . it'll last longer

Visualizing what a story looks, sounds, and smells like in your mind is one of the most magical parts of reading, especially once kids get to books that don't include very many illustrations. But building a mental picture of events can help you comprehend nonfiction texts and school assignments, too. Encourage kids to always think actively as they read, trying to imagine exactly what all those sentences mean. If your mind loses focus, you could find yourself missing information—even if you're technically reading every word. (As anyone who has ever had to go back and read, reread, and re-reread a single textbook paragraph knows!)

Stop and summarize the roses

Pause every once in a while to review the story and think about what you understand. If you notice that some part of the text is unclear, go forward or backward in the story to fill yourself in on what you're missing.

Put yourself on the page

One of the most effective ways to understand new information is to relate it to something you already know. Encourage kids to think about how they can connect what they're reading to their own real-life experiences. Like if you're reading a book about boats, talk about the time your family went on a boat together, and discuss how your experience was the same as or different from the book. Or if you're reading one of Shannon and Dean Hale's *Princess in Black* books, remind your kid of the time you had to defend your family goat against a monster who emerged from a hole and tried to eat it. (If applicable.)

Gimme a "why"

In school, students will need to be able to reference textbooks and other assigned reading in order to answer comprehension questions. Kids can get practice with this by telling you about the books they're reading now. Start by asking questions like: "What do you think was the most important part of the book?" "What was the main character like?" and "What do you think the moral of the story was?" Then follow up each of those questions with, "Why?" Encourage your bookmonster to move beyond responses like "I don't know" or "It just seems that way to me," and instead think of real examples from the story that support their answers. Doing so will increase your kiddo's confidence, and help them come to a deeper understanding and appreciation of the things they read.

Dramatizing text

After bookmonsters are comfortable identifying and understanding the words on the page, they will be free to take one last leap toward becoming truly eloquent and impassioned readers. What is that leap, you ask? *Dramatizing* what they read. The ability to read with mean-ingful expression that communicates a thorough understanding of all the emotions at stake is what transports readers from the tedious task of reciting rote words off a page to the energizing experience of bring-ing books to life.

Once you see your kid acting out scenes from favorite books, or mimicking characters' facial expressions, or dramatically delivering lines of dialogue *just for fun*, you'll know they've caught the reading bug. And with your continued support, creativity, and encouragement, they will never, ever lose it. Here are ways to make that happen:

Read it once more, with feeling

In our "The Right Way to Read to a Bookmonster" chapter (page 54), we recommend that you use plenty of emotion when reading with your kid. As children begin doing more of the reading themselves, it's a good idea to encourage them to read with feeling, too. If you ever sense that they're concentrating too much on just getting through the words, and as a result sound like choppy, emotionless sci-fi show robots, try "rebooting" their systems. Say something like, "Hey, that was really great, but I just thought of something that would make it even more fun! What if you read that last sentence again, but this time, say it how you think that evil, mutant, criminal mastermind ostrich character who is trying to take over the world would *actually* say it!"

Allow kids to act up

Since kids love to pretend, they will sometimes spontaneously act out the stories they read. When they do, you can promote this behavior by taking a moment to be an attentive and appreciative audience.

While reading the truly magical Doll People series by Ann M. Martin and Laura Godwin, our kids were motivated to set up their own dollhouse and have adventures with it. They also pretended they were dolls themselves, following the rules set out in the books: They could talk and move when people weren't watching them, but if someone saw them they'd be rendered motionless, briefly stuck in a statue-like "doll state." Our kids had a blast freezing, reanimating, and trying to "catch" each other moving. Plus playing this way helped them better understand and empathize with the characters as we read.

Make funny faces

When a character in a book is described as making an interesting face, feeling a particular emotion, or speaking or moving in an unusually expressive way, ask your kid to try doing it, too. We do this with our family all the time, and the kids absolutely slay each other (and us) trying to perform the most outrageous version of whatever we just read. And you don't even need a book to get started. Just pick a feeling—surprised, mad, sad, aghast, deep-in-thought, or whatever you can dream up—then tell your little one to show you that face. Adorbs!

Try some twinning

Imitating other people is a simple enough activity that babies can do it, yet it's also fun for older kids and adults. Just sit or stand facing another person, then try to copycat their exact movements, like you're looking in a mirror. Be sure to take turns being the leader, and increase the challenge by trying to reproduce not just movements, but also facial expressions, emotions, words, sounds, songs, making a dove appear out of a magic hat, or whatever else you want!

Put on a play

Show kids how fun it is to perform by encouraging them to plan and act out their own plays at home. They can write an original story, use scripts from children's play books like *Cinderella Outgrows the Glass Slipper and Other Zany Fractured Fairy Tale Plays* by J. M. Wolf, or re-create tales they already know like "Goldilocks and the Three Bears." Bigger kids can take larger speaking parts (like Goldilocks), while tiny kids take non-speaking roles (like The Porridge). Some families even make traditions out of creating play productions whenever they have holiday gatherings. Maybe yours could, too!

Bookmonsters Can Overcome Anything

Congratulations, you did it—you've journeyed deep into the heart and mind of your child and found the elusive bookmonster hiding within. You've learned how to care for it, feed it, work with it, and play with it, and now you've got a thriving specimen on your hands. Looks like your job here is done.

Just kidding!

Your story doesn't end when you reach the last page of this book, and it doesn't even end when your child becomes an independent reader. Truth be told, this raising-a-bookmonster thing that you've gotten yourself into is a totally long-term gig. Over the next few years, there will still be lots to learn, practice, improve upon, and master, so be sure to stay involved with your kid's literary growth and continue to use reading as a way to live, laugh, and love together. When you do that, bringing up your child as a bookmonster can be one of the most rewarding things you'll do—for both of you!

We have to be honest, though: it *won't* always be easy. Incorporating as many books and conversations as possible into your family's life sounds like a simple mandate, so you may be shocked to learn that finding the right routine for your particular bookmonster brood will probably take some fiddling. We're talking lots of trial and error, people. Plus plenty of potential pitfalls along the way. Here are just a few that you may run into:

Running into things while attempting to walk and read at the same time

Once your child falls for reading, they'll want to do it anywhere and everywhere, including when they're en route between two places—which can result in them *literally* falling for reading. Like the time our first grader and her friend were trying to walk while utterly engrossed in *Walt Disney Treasury: Donald Duck Volume 1* by Don Rosa. Both of them took a tumble down a mini flight of three stairs before they ever looked up from their book.

Reading during mealtime

We knew we wanted to establish some family book-reading routines, so when someone told us that they loved to read picture books to their young kids during meals, we thought it would be a cool thing to do in our house. Until we tried it and found that reading at the table kept us from connecting through conversations about our day. Since then, we've also discovered that allowing kids to read their own books independently at the table has the same negative effect on interaction. So now we're careful to ban books along with other distractions like technology and toys from the table, only making exceptions when our whole family is enjoying a multi-chapter read-aloud together.

Shirking responsibilities

Shrewd little bookmonsters who realize just how important books are to their families might try to use reading as an excuse for avoiding chores, homework, bedtime, or other responsibilities. We know it can be tough to tear your bookmonster away from books and their myriad benefits. But don't worry, your kiddo can get right back to reading after the dishes have been put away.

Poor eyesight

Concerned that holding books mere inches from their eyeballs all day will cause kids to need glasses? You're not the only one. Good thing bookmonsters know how to have fun with language and literacy in all sorts of ways, both with and without books. Be sure to get your kid outside frequently, since research shows that spending time in sunlight may help prevent the onset of nearsightedness and slow its progression—no matter how much time kids spend with their noses in a book!

Papercuts

Ouch. Be careful out there, bookmonsters!

Running out of shelf space

This one hits close to home for us, because we live in an urban area where living space is at an absolute premium. So we've maximized unused wall space by building additional bookshelves, co-opted parts of our linen and game closets to find more places for books, and made a point of going through our stuff every six months or so to get rid of things we're no longer using. (We're talking about you, bag of broken seashells and crappy kids' meal toys!)

Using tons of tape

When bookmonsters are little, they're rough on books. Infants stick them in their mouths, so books made from durable materials like the Workman Publishing Company's Indestructibles books are a wise investment. Toddlers tear flaps and pages galore before mastering the art of being gentle. And even older kids can't avoid an accidental rip every now and then. So you'll want to have lots of tape on hand for book repairs. When our oldest bookmonster was four, she had gotten so used to the tape repair routine that she took it upon herself to fix a badly torn page she discovered in a library book she'd just checked out. We only found out about her operation later, when a librarian told us that our family had been banned from checking out more books because of it! Apparently our daughter's attempted repair job was misconstrued as vandalism, because in addition to making it look like a four-year-old did it, she had also inadvertently used double-sided tape—which made an even bigger mess of the situation.

Losing sleep

Our son has literally lost sleep over books. Not because he was reading them under his covers with a flashlight like you'd expect, but because he was simply *thinking* about them. One night he reported that he wasn't able to sleep because he couldn't stop thinking about how much he wanted the *Dog Man* book by Dav Pilkey he heard was coming out in a few months. We told him that we had already preordered it and he would get it as soon as it was available—so stop thinking about it and sleep already. After a few minutes he emerged from his room again, telling us that now he couldn't sleep because he was so excited to know that he definitely *will* get it!

Losing innocence

Because bookmonsters frequently read above their grade levels, they sometimes get exposed to content they're not ready for. Like the time our elementary school–age daughter read *All's Faire in Middle School* by Victoria Jamieson—a graphic novel with cute illustrations and an accessible storyline, but also some romantic themes that were too mature for her at the time. Even when you're reading aloud to your child, you may run into words your family doesn't use—like "hate" or "stupid"—which you'll have to think fast to censor. To check books for content, try skimming the synopses and being extra cautious about book characters who are much older or in more advanced grades than your child.

Making unpredictable progress

If you're worried that your child isn't advancing fast enough, understand that bringing up a bookmonster will help inspire a long-lasting love of literacy, but it won't be instantaneous. All kids reach language and literacy milestones at different times, and you never know when your unique kiddo is going to put the pieces together. Try to be patient, and rest assured that each of the conversations and book reading sessions you and your child enjoy will encourage them on their way. But if you're still concerned, don't hesitate to bring it up with your child's pediatrician. (They usually have some amazing books in the waiting room, too!)

You'll undoubtedly experience these issues differently than our family has, and you'll surely discover some unexpected challenges of your own. But let that be part of the fun. Pretty soon you'll have your own stories about the delightful things your kid has said during book reading, and the unexpected ways your family has been banned from your own local library.

It's been an honor to act as your guides through the unforgettable process of uncovering your child's inner bookmonster. Although you'll always have this book to refer to, there may be times when you run into situations that we haven't specifically covered here. Maybe you'll find a new "brain-boosting" app or "must-have" reading toy, or come upon some unforeseen literacy or parenting issue. When this happens, we hope you remember the core lessons we've communicated throughout this book:

> *Talk to your kid.*
> *Read to your kid.*
> *Have fun doing both!*

If you can remember to do those things as much as possible, more often than not, and whenever you might be in doubt, then you and your bookmonster will always find your way.

Notes

Introduction: The Bookmonster Right Under Your Nose

Kids who love language

G. J. Duncan et al.,"School readiness and later achievement." *Developmental Psychology* 43, no. 6 (2007): 1428–46.

kids who were read to

M. Sénéchal and J. LeFevre, "Storybook reading and parent teaching: Links to language and literacy development" in *New Directions for Child and Adolescent Development: The Role of Family Literacy Environments in Promoting Young Children's Emerging Literacy Skills*, eds. P. R. Britto and J. Brooks-Gunn (San Francisco: Jossey-Bass, 2001), 39–52.

1: Anatomy of a Bookmonster

fetuses and young children

L. L. Torres, et al., "Tobacco Smoke and Nicotine: Neurotoxicity in Brain Development," in *Addictive Substances and Neurological Disease*, eds. Ronald Watson and Shirma Zibadi (Cambridge, MA: Academic Press, 2017) 273–80.

Learning to read requires

P. E. Turkeltaub et al., "Development of neural mechanisms for reading," *Nature Neuroscience* 6, no. 7 (2003): 767.

M. Wolf, and C. J. Stoodley, *Proust and the Squid: The Story and Science of the Reading Brain* (New York: Harper Perennial, 2008).

Children who are read to

J. E. Adrian et al., "Parent-child picture-book reading, mothers' mental state language and children's theory of mind," *Journal of Child Language* 32, no. 3 (2005): 673–86.

adults who read more frequently

D. C. Kidd and E. Castano, "Reading literary fiction improves theory of mind," *Science* 342, no. 6156 (2013): 377–80.

2: The Perfect Bookmonster Call

some kids hear up to thirty million

B. Hart and T. R. Risley, *Meaningful Differences in the Everyday Experience of Young American Children* (Baltimore: Paul H. Brookes Publishing, 1995).

Kids who have heard more words

P. L. Morgan et al., "24-month-old children with larger oral vocabularies display greater academic and behavioral functioning at kindergarten entry," *Child Development* 86, no. 5 (2015): 1351–70.

Children with larger vocabularies

G. J. Duncan et al., "School readiness and later achievement," *Developmental Psychology* 43, no. 6 (2007): 1428–46.

having at least five family dinners

S. M. Fruh, et al., "The surprising benefits of the family meal," *The Journal for Nurse Practitioners* 7, no. 1 (2011): 18–22.

3: Listening to a Bookmonster

kids whose parents responded more

C. S. Tamis-LeMonda, M. H. Bornstein, and L. Baumwell, "Maternal responsiveness and children's achievement of language milestones," *Child Development* 72, no. 3 (2001): 748–67.

Children whose parents provided responses

M. H. Goldstein and J. A. Schwade, "Social feedback to infants' babbling facilitates rapid phonological learning," *Psychological Science* 19, no. 5 (2008): 515–23.

Because there is no reliable response

A. T. Smyke et al., "The caregiving context in institution-reared and family-reared infants and toddlers in Romania," *Journal of Child Psychology and Psychiatry* 48, no. 2 (2007): 210–18.

kids learn most from conversations

N. Akhtar, F. Dunham, and P. J. Dunham, "Directive interactions and early vocabulary development: The role of joint attentional focus," *Journal of Child Language* 18, no.1 (1991): 41–49.

kids actively interacting with parents

M. Chouinard, P. Harris, and M. Maratsos, "Children's Questions: A Mechanism for Cognitive Development," *Monographs of the Society for Research in Child Development* 72, no.1 (2007): 1–129.

4: Moving Like a Bookmonster

without guidance to pay attention

L. M. Justice, P. C. Pullen, and K. Pence, "Influence of Verbal and Nonverbal References to Print on Preschoolers' Visual Attention to Print During Storybook Reading," *Developmental Psychology* 44, no. 3 (2008): 855.

the opposite is true

S. W. Goodwyn, L. P. Acredolo, and C. A. Brown, "Impact of Symbolic Gesturing on Early Language Development," *Journal of Nonverbal Behavior* 24, no. 2 (2000): 81–103.

5: The Right Time to Read to a Bookmonster

shared reading teaches

R. Indrisano and J. S. Chall, "Literacy Development," *Journal of Education* 177, no. 1 (1995): 63–83.

This is particularly important to help

J. S. Chall and V. A. Jacobs, "The Classic Study on Poor Children's Fourth-Grade Slump," *American Educator* 27, no. 1 (2003): 14–15.

reading a book at bedtime has benefits

L. Hale et al., "A Longitudinal Study of Preschoolers' Language-Based Bedtime Routines, Sleep Duration, and Well-Being," *Journal of Family Psychology* 25, no. 3 (2011): 423.

Families that do this fare better

J. A. Mindell et al., "A Nightly Bedtime Routine: Impact on Sleep in Young Children and Maternal Mood," *Sleep* 32, no. 5 (2009): 599–606.

something called the "summer reading setback"

D. B. Downey, P. T. Von Hippel, and B. A. Broh, "Are Schools the Great Equalizer? Cognitive Inequality During the Summer Months and the School Year," *American Sociological Review* 69, no. 5 (2004): 613–35.

6: The Right Way to Read to a Bookmonster

comparison is a particularly effective way

A. A. Ankowski, H. A. Vlach, and C. M. Sandhofer, "Comparison Versus Contrast: Task Specifics Affect Category Acquisition," *Infant and Child Development* 22, no. 1 (2013): 1–23.

7: Setting a Bookmonster Trap

children whose homes contained

M. D. Evans, J. Kelley, and J. Sikora, "Scholarly Culture and Academic Performance in 42 Nations," *Social Forces* 92, no. 4 (2014): 1573–1605.

people perform better when they are tested

S. M. Smith and E. Vela, "Environmental Context-Dependent Memory: A Review and Meta-Analysis," *Psychonomic Bulletin & Review* 8, no. 2 (2001): 203–20.

kids performed significantly better

H. A. Vlach and C. M. Sandhofer, "Developmental Differences in Children's Context-Dependent Word Learning," *Journal of Experimental Child Psychology* 108 (2011): 394–401.

E. R. Goldenberg and C. M. Sandhofer, "Same, Varied, or Both? Contextual Support Aids Young Children in Generalizing Category Labels," *Journal of Experimental Child Psychology* 115, no.1 (2013): 150–62.

10: Screen Time for Bookmonsters

children ages 0 to 8

V. Rideout, "The Common Sense Census: Media Use by Kids Age Zero to Eight," ed. M. Robb, Common Sense Media (2017).

Exposure to too much non-educational television

B. Huber et al., "The Effects of Screen Media Content on Young Children's Executive Functioning," *Journal of Experimental Child Psychology* 170 (2018): 72–85.

Even when the screen

G. A. Strouse, and J. E. Samson, "Learning from Video: A Meta-Analysis of the Video Deficit in Children Ages 0 to 6 Years," *Child Development* (2020).

the effect of in-bedroom screens

D. A. Gentile et al., "Bedroom Media: One Risk Factor for Development," *Developmental Psychology* 53, no.12 (2017): 2340–55.

your interaction with another person

B. T. McDaniel and J. S. Radesky, "Technoference: Parent Distraction with Technology and Associations with Child Behavior Problems," *Child Development* 89, no. 1 (2018): 100–9.

families did significantly less

H. L. Kirkorian et al., "The Impact of Background Television on Parent-Child Interaction" *Child Development* 80, no. 5 (2009): 1350–59.

families who frequently have the television on

E. F. Masur, V. Flynn, and J. Olson, "Infants' Background Television Exposure During Play: Negative Relations to the Quantity and Quality of Mothers' Speech and Infants' Vocabulary Acquisition," *First Language* 36, no. 2 (2016): 109–23.

One of the biggest predictors
E. Wartella et al., *Parenting in the Age of Digital Technology*, Center on Media and Human Development School of Communication, Northwestern University (2013).

kids can learn some pretty cool stuff
P. M. Greenfield, "Technology and Informal Education: What Is Taught, What Is Learned," *Science* 323, no. 5910 (2009): 69–71.

they can lead to higher levels
C. A. Anderson et al., "Violent Video Game Effects on Aggression, Empathy, and Prosocial Behavior in Eastern and Western Countries: A Meta-Analytic Review," *Psychological Bulletin* 136, no. 2 (2010): 151.

when a true interactive element
S. Roseberry, K. Hirsh-Pasek, and R. M. Golinkoff, "Skype Me! Socially Contingent Interactions Help Toddlers Learn Language," *Child development* 85, no. 3 (2014): 956–70.

when technology is involved
M. Krcmar and D. P. Cingel, "Parent-Child Joint Reading in Traditional and Electronic Formats," *Media Psychology* 17, no. 3 (2014): 262–81.

both kids and adults struggle
A. Mangen, B. R. Walgermo, and K. Brønnick, "Reading Linear Texts on Paper Versus Computer Screen: Effects on Reading Comprehension," *International Journal of Educational Research* 58 (2013): 61–68.

11: Playtime for Bookmonsters

no lasting advantage for kids
K. Hirsh-Pasek, M. C. Hyson, and L. Rescorla, "Academic Environments in Preschool: Do They Pressure or Challenge Young Children," *Early Education and Development* 1, no. 6 (1990): 401–23.

children from families who engage
S. M. Fruh, "The Surprising Benefits of the Family Meal," *The Journal for Nurse Practitioners* 7, no.1 (2011): 18–22.

pretend play promotes higher-level thinking skills
D. Bergen, "The Role of Pretend Play in Children's Cognitive Development," *Early Childhood Research & Practice* 4, no. 1 (2002): n1.

12: Bookmonsters Travel in Packs

kids who read more
J. E. Adrian, "Parent-Child Picture-Book Reading, Mothers' Mental State Language and Children's Theory of Mind," *Journal of Child Language* 323 (2005): 673–86.

The connection between more reading
R. A. Mar, K. Oatley, and J. B. Peterson, "Exploring the Link Between Reading Fiction and Empathy: Ruling Out Individual Differences and Examining Outcomes," *Communications* 34, no. 4 (2009): 407–28.

13: The Best Books for Your Bookmonster

when families read humorous books
E. Hoicka, S. Jutsum, and M. Gattis, "Humor, Abstraction, and Disbelief," *Cognitive Science* 32, no. 6 (2008): 985–1002.

introducing children to STEM concepts
R. Dou et al., "Early Informal STEM Experiences and STEM Identity: The Importance of Talking Science," *Science Education* 103, no. 3 (2019): 623–37.

14: Speaking a Bookmonster's Language

phonological awareness is one of the two
J. K. Torgesen, R. K. Wagner, and C. A. Rashotte, "Longitudinal Studies of Phonological Processing and Reading," *Journal of Learning Disabilities* 27, no. 5 (1994): 276–86.

Amassing a large vocabulary
J. Lee, "Size Matters: Early Vocabulary as a Predictor of Language and Literacy Competence," *Applied Psycholinguistics* 32, no. 1 (2011): 69.

a strong connection between familiarity
P. E. Bryant et al., "Nursery Rhymes, Phonological Skills and Reading," *Journal of Child Language* 16, no. 2 (1989): 407–28.

16: The Magic of a Bookmonster's Name

people end up disproportionately marrying
J. T. Jones, "How Do I Love Thee? Let Me Count the Js: Implicit Egotism and Interpersonal Attraction," *Journal of Personality and Social Psychology* 87, no. 5 (2004): 665.

conversations last significantly longer
R. Treiman et al., "Parents' Talk About Letters with Their Young Children," *Child Development* 86, no. 5 (2015): 1406–18.

kids whose parents use
R. Treiman et al., "Parents' Talk About Letters with Their Young Children," *Child Development* 86, no. 5 (2015): 1406–18.

17: Bookmonsters Like Laughing

children with more developed senses of humor

W. E. Hauck and J. W. Thomas, "The Relationship of Humor to Intelligence, Creativity, and Intentional and Incidental Learning," *The Journal of Experimental Education* 40, no. 4 (1972): 52–55.

E. Hoicka, S. Jutsum, and M. Gattis, "Humor, Abstraction, and Disbelief," *Cognitive Science* 32, no. 6 (2008): 985–1002.

people tend to remember humorous lessons

M. G. Lovorn, "Humor in the Home and in the Classroom: The Benefits of Laughing while we Learn," *Journal of Education and Human Development* 2, no. 1 (2008).

18: Two-Tongued Bookmonsters

this extra effort pays off

J. Morales, A. Calvo, and E. Bialystok, "Working Memory Development in Monolingual and Bilingual Children," *Journal of Experimental Child Psychology* 114, no. 2 (2012): 187–202.

being bilingual delays the onset

S. Alladi et al., "Bilingualism Delays Age at Onset of Dementia, Independent of Education and Immigration Status," *Neurology* 81, no. 22 (2013): 1938–44.

After hearing the language

P. K. Kuhl, F. M. Tsao, and H. M. Liu, "Foreign-Language Experience in Infancy: Effects of Short-Term Exposure and Social Interaction on Phonetic Learning," *Proceedings of the National Academy of Sciences* 100, no.15 (2003): 9096–101.

20: Bookmonsters Love to Write

children who are read to more often

R. Lever and M. Sénéchal, "Discussing Stories: On How a Dialogic Reading Intervention Improves Kindergartners' Oral Narrative Construction," *Journal of Experimental Child Psychology* 108, no. 1 (2011): 1–24.

Children who experienced interactive reading

V. Purcell-Gates, "Lexical and Syntactic Knowledge of Written Narrative Held by Well-Read-to Kindergartners and Second Graders," *Research in the Teaching of English* (1988): 128–60.

when college students take handwritten notes

P. A. Mueller and D. M. Oppenheimer, "The Pen is Mightier than the Keyboard: Advantages of Longhand over Laptop Note Taking," *Psychological Science* 25, no. 6 (1988): 1159–68.

kids who can write faster

D. Jones, and C. A. Christensen, "Relationship Between Automaticity in Handwriting and Students' Ability to Generate Written Text," *Journal of Educational Psychology* 91, no. 1 (1999): 44.

S. T. Peverly et al., "The Relationship of Handwriting Speed, Working Memory, Language Comprehension and Outlines to Lecture Note-Taking and Test-Taking Among College Students," *Applied Cognitive Psychology* 27, no. 1 (2013): 115–26.

faster writers are less likely

H. Van Waelvelde et al., "SOS: A Screening Instrument to Identify Children with Handwriting Impairments," *Physical & Occupational Therapy in Pediatrics* 32, no. 3 (2012): 306–19.

the specific pencil grip

J. Ziviani and J. Elkins, "Effect of Pencil Grip on Handwriting Speed and Legibility," *Educational Review* 38, no. 3 (1986): 247–57.

copying letters in this way

M. Longcamp, M. T. Zerbato-Poudou, and J. L. Velay, "The Influence of Writing Practice on Letter Recognition in Preschool Children: A Comparison Between Handwriting and Typing," *Acta psychologica* 119, no. 1 (2005): 67–79.

21: Bookmonsters Go Wild for Weird Words

In the late 1970s

A. Senghas, "Intergenerational Influence and Ontogenetic Development in the Emergence of Spatial Grammar in Nicaraguan Sign Language," *Cognitive Development* 18, no. 4 (2003): 511–31.

23: Bookmonsters Sweat the Small Stuff

there are cross-cultural differences

M. Carr et al., "Strategy Acquisition and Transfer Among American and German Children: Environmental Influences on Metacognitive Development," *Developmental Psychology* 25, no. 5 (1989): 765.

Conclusion: Bookmonsters Can Overcome Anything

spending time in sunlight

J. C. Sherwin et al., "The Association Between Time Spent Outdoors and Myopia in Children and Adolescents: a Systematic Review and Meta-Analysis," *Ophthalmology* 119, no. 10 (2012): 2141–51.

Bookshelf

Ready to start reading with your bookmonster? Here's a list of all the children's books we mentioned throughout this book, organized by Book Pyramid category (see page 130). Remember that many books can belong to more than one category, and that "Unique interests" could contain any book at all, as long as your bookmonster finds it interesting!

Literacy skill building

Amelia Bedelia by Peggy Parish (page 60)

Ann and Nan Are Anagrams: A Mixed-Up Word Dilemma by Mark Shulman (page 209)

Beastly Feasts! by Robert L. Forbes (page 131)

Bert & Ernie's First Book of Opposites by Heather Au (page 48)

Big Little and *Yummy Yucky* by Leslie Patricelli (page 207)

Brown Bear, Brown Bear, What Do You See? by Bill Martin Jr. and Eric Carle (page 56)

Bunny Cakes by Rosemary Wells (page 199)

Dinosaur Roar! by Paul and Henrietta Stickland (page 132)

Fancy Nancy series by Jane O'Connor (page 132)

Fancy Nancy: Ooh La La! It's Beauty Day by Jane O'Connor (page 124)

First 100 Words by Roger Priddy (page 132)

Go, Dog. Go! by P. D. Eastman (page 149)

Goodnight, Goodnight, Construction Site by Sherri Duskey Rinker (page 219)

The Goodnight Train by June Sobel (page 151)

Green Eggs and Ham by Dr. Seuss (page 131)

I'm Just No Good at Rhyming: And Other Nonsense for Mischievous Kids and Immature Grown-Ups by Chris Harris (page 131)

The Indestructibles books from Workman Publishing (page 246)

Jeepers Creepers: A Monstrous ABC by Laura Leuck (page 131)

Little Blue Truck by Alice Schertle (page 209)

The My Big Wimmelbooks series from The Experiment (page 58)

Nanette's Baguette by Mo Willems (page 206)

No No Yes Yes by Leslie Patricelli (page 207)

Oh Say Can You Say? by Dr. Seuss (page 213)

On Top of Spaghetti by Paul Brett Johnson (page 204)

One Dark Night by Hazel Hutchins (page 208)

The Original Mother Goose illustrated by Blanche Fisher Wright (page 151)

Peanut Butter & Cupcake! by Terry Border (page 226)

The Pout-Pout Fish by Deborah Diesen (page 131)

Skippyjon Jones by Judy Schachner (page 132)

The Sleepy Little Alphabet by Judy Sierra (page 149)

Smart Feller Fart Smeller by Jon Agee (page 214)

Thesaurus Rex by Laya Steinberg (page 207)

The Timmy Failure series by Stephan Pastis (page 132)

Where the Sidewalk Ends by Shel Silverstein (page 131)

Which Way to Witch School? by Scott Santoro (page 207)

The Word Collector by Peter H. Reynolds (page 132)

Just for fun

Adventures in Cartooning by James Sturm, Andrew Arnold, and Alexis Frederick-Frost (page 134)

The Adventures of Super Diaper Baby by Dav Pilkey (page 134)

The Captain Underpants series by Dav Pilkey (page 107)

Captain Underpants and the Attack of the Talking Toilets by Dav Pilkey (page 210)

The Days Are Just Packed: A Calvin and Hobbes Collection by Bill Watterson (page 134)

Dog Man by Dav Pilkey (page 246)

Garfield at Large by Jim Davis (page 134)

Hello Kitty: Delicious! by Jorge Monlongo (page 134)

The Just Joking series from National Geographic Kids (page 133)

Laugh-Out-Loud Animal Jokes for Kids by Rob Elliott (page 133)

Martha Speaks: Funny Bone Jokes and Riddles by Karen Barss and Susan Meddaugh (page 133)

More Bears! by Kenn Nesbitt (page 135)

Narwhal: Unicorn of the Sea by Ben Clanton (page 134)

Press Here by Hervé Tullet (page 135)

Riddles & Brain Teasers: Best Riddles for Challenging Smart Kids by Rusty Cove-Smith (page 133)

Snappsy the Alligator (Did Not Ask to Be in This Book) by Julie Falatko (page 135)

The Super, Epic, Mega Joke Book for Kids by Whee Winn (page 133)

This Book Just Ate My Dog! by Richard Byrne (page 135)

We Are in a Book! by Mo Willems (page 135)

Learning lessons

The Atlas Obscura Explorer's Guide for the World's Most Adventurous Kid by Dylan Thuras and Rosemary Mosco (page 137)

Big Magic for Little Hands by Joshua Jay (page 140)

Botanicum: Welcome to the Museum by Katie Scott and Kathy Willis (page 252)

The Boy Who Loved Math: The Improbable Life of Paul Erdos by Deborah Heiligman (page 252)

Cinderella Outgrows the Glass Slipper and Other Zany Fractured Fairy Tale Plays by J. M. Wolf (page 242)

Crafting with Cat Hair: Cute Handicrafts to Make with Your Cat by Kaori Tsutaya (page 252)

The Curious Kids' Science Book: 100+ Creative Hands-On Activities for Ages 4–8 by Asia Citro (page 218)

Don't Let the Pigeon Finish This Activity Book! by Mo Willems (page 138)

Easy Origami by John Montroll (page 138)

Flush!: The Scoop on Poop Throughout the Ages by Charise Mericle Harper (page 137)

Grandma's Tiny House by JaNay Brown-Wood (page 136)

The Gross Cookbook by Susanna Tee (page 219)

The I Survived series by Lauren Tarshis (page 138)

Iggy Peck, Architect by Andrea Beaty (page 66)

Ivy + Bean + Me: A Fill-in-the-Blank Book by Annie Barrows (page 138)

Kid Chef Bakes: The Kids Cookbook for Aspiring Bakers by Lisa Huff (page 219)

Kitchen Science Lab for Kids: 52 Family-Friendly Experiments from Around the House by Liz Lee Heinecke (page 136)

The LEGO Ideas Book: Unlock Your Imagination by Daniel Lipkowitz (page 219)

Let's Explore a Pirate Ship by Nicholas Harris (page 138)

The Lives of . . . series by Kathleen Krull and Kathryn Hewitt (page 138)

The Mad Libs series from Penguin Random House (page 137)

Moon! Earth's Best Friend by Stacy McAnulty (page 218)

Storybooks

Big Foot and Little Foot by Ellen Potter (page 142)

Bread and Jam for Frances by Russell Hoban (page 254)

Busy, Busy Town by Richard Scarry (page 59)

Cam Jansen and the Tennis Trophy Mystery by David A. Adler (page 116)

Charlie and the Cheese Monster by Justin C. H. Birch (page 17)

Charlie and the Chocolate Factory by Roald Dahl (page 106)

The Chronicles of Narnia series by C. S. Lewis (page 142)

Click, Clack, Moo: Cows that Type by Doreen Cronin (page 140)

Cloudy with a Chance of Meatballs by Judi Barrett (page 254)

Doctor Proctor's Fart Powder by Jo Nesbø (page 140)

The Doll People series by Ann M. Martin and Laura Godwin (page 241)

Flora and the Flamingo by Molly Idle (page 58)

Gangsta Granny by David Walliams (page 142)

The Gingerbread Man by Jim Aylesworth (page 41)

Goldilocks and the Three Bears as retold by Jim Aylesworth (page 144)

Goodnight Moon by Margaret Wise Brown (page 144)

Guess How Much I Love You by Sam McBratney (page 45)

The Harry Potter series by J. K. Rowling (page 107)

The Hoboken Chicken Emergency by Daniel Pinkwater (page 77)

Holes by Louis Sachar (page 107)

How Do You Feel? by Anthony Browne (page 141)

I Love You, Daddy by Jillian Harker (page 48)

I Will Take a Nap! by Mo Willems (page 40)

I'm Not Moving! by Wiley Blevins (page 141)

The Indian in the Cupboard by Lynne Reid Banks (page 142)

James and the Giant Peach by Roald Dahl (page 77)

Judy Moody, M.D.: The Doctor Is In! by Megan McDonald (page 209)

The Land of Stories series by Chris Colfer (page 140)

The Lion and the Little Red Bird by Elisa Kleven (page 69)

Unique interests

Further Reading

Want to read more about raising readers? Here are some of the most accessible and commercially available resources we referenced while writing this book.

Child Development by Laura Berk

Children's Thinking: Cognitive Development and Individual Differences by David Bjorklund and Kayla Causey

Language Development by Erika Hoff

Meaningful Differences in the Everyday Experience of Young American Children by Betty Hart and Todd Risley

Media Moms & Digital Dads: A Fact-Not-Fear Approach to Parenting in the Digital Age by Yalda Uhls

The New Childhood: Raising Kids to Thrive in a Connected World by Jordan Shapiro

NurtureShock: New Thinking About Children by Po Bronson and Ashley Merryman

Proust and the Squid: The Story and Science of the Reading Brain by Maryanne Wolf

Reader, Come Home: The Reading Brain in a Digital World by Maryanne Wolf

The Read-Aloud Family: Making Meaningful and Lasting Connections with Your Kids by Sarah Mackenzie

Think Like a Baby: 33 Simple Research Experiments You Can Do at Home to Better Understand Your Child's Developing Mind by Amber Ankowski, PhD, and Andy Ankowski

Index

Acknowledgments

Thank you to our children, Sammy, Freddy, and Millie, for giving us a reason to write this book, filling its pages with amazing anecdotes and showing us how fantastically ferocious three bookmonsters can be.

Thank you to our parents, Mary Jo and Jim Ankowski and Jack and Karen Aguiar, for raising us to love reading so we could inspire our kids to do the same. Thank you to our siblings, Nicole Harvilla, Jason Aguiar, Heather Udell, and Kristin Davies, for sharing countless stories with us throughout the years.

Thank you to TJ and Ashleigh Sochor, Chris and Emily Russell, Ashley Kulik, and Peter Kavelin, who helped us first envision what the bookmonster species might look like. Thank you to Jen Prakash for reading early drafts of our manuscript, and to Erin Vail, Megan Baltruzak, and Mary Aguiar for inspiring some of our tips.

Thank you to all the teachers who have been so influential to our family, including those who taught us, especially Sherie Segler, Peggy

Oxley, and Bill Kerwin, and those who have taught our children, especially Edward Curry, whose tireless and joyful approach toward getting kids to read is truly inspiring, and Krikor Mesrobian, who enthusiastically energizes students to maintain their love of reading (and who motivated our family's love of Harry Potter).

Thank you to Amber's professional colleagues and mentors who have been crucial to helping her acquire the experience and expertise needed to write this book, especially Cathy Sandhofer, who has been there every step of the way.

Thank you to our agent, Uwe Stender, whose passion for our work keeps us writing, and to Batya Rosenblum, Hannah Matuszak, and everyone at The Experiment, for allowing us to discover where this bookmonster expedition would take us!

About the Authors

AMBER ANKOWSKI, PHD, teaches psychology at the University of California, Los Angeles, with a focus on children's language and cognitive development and methods for conducting psychological research. Her work has been published in academic journals including *Child Development Research*, *Infant and Child Development*, and *Journal of Experimental Psychology: Learning, Memory, and Cognition.*

ANDY ANKOWSKI is an award-winning advertising creative director who specializes in explaining complex products and services in simple—and often laugh-out-loud funny—ways. He studied creative writing at the University of Notre Dame, and once wrote 365 poems about onion bagels in a single year.

Together, they are parenting speakers, bloggers at doctoranddad.com, authors of *Think Like a Baby: 33 Simple Research Experiments You Can Do at Home to Better Understand Your Child's Developing Mind* and *Goodnight Zoom,* and parents of three fantastically ferocious bookmonsters.

doctoranddad.com